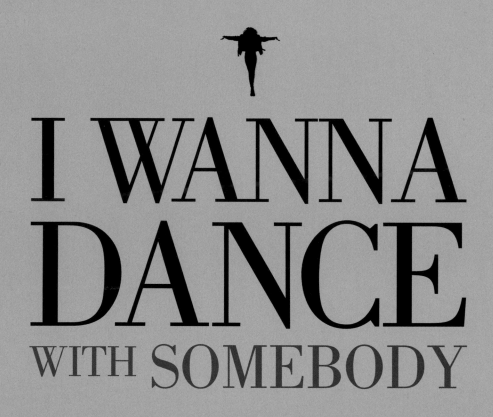

I WANNA DANCE

WITH SOMEBODY

THE OFFICIAL WHITNEY HOUSTON FILM COMPANION

SIMON WARD

FOREWORD BY NAOMI ACKIE

weldon**owen**

CONTENTS

Previous page and left: Naomi Ackie
as Whitney Houston.

Following page: Whitney Houston
performing in Paris Bercy on
May 18, 1988.

Dedicated to Whitney
and to all of those
who love her.

FOREWORD
BY NAOMI ACKIE

I can't quite believe I'm writing these words. It's been a long, long time since my agent got the call and told me I had the part of a lifetime—playing Whitney Houston in the official story of her life. That was in 2020. I still remember drinking champagne on the floor with my agent, celebrating, and thinking about the adventure ahead.

It was fall 2021 before I actually came on set as Whitney for the first time. With the wonderful team around me on that movie, it wouldn't be right to say I felt pressure, but I certainly did feel responsibility. Whitney Houston is loved the world over and her music has touched so many. I wanted to honor her. Everyone on the film felt the same. From my director, Kasi, the producers, Denis, Anthony, Jeff, Clive Davis, Larry Mestel, and Pat Houston, to all the dedicated crew and the amazing Polly Bennet, who helped bring the film to life and gave me the courage to step into Whitney's shoes.

The book you're holding in your hands is a record of how we made this movie. For me, it's like looking at a photo album of the last two years of my life—a life I shared with Whitney. I hope you enjoy the book as much as we enjoyed making *I Wanna Dance with Somebody*.

And as for Whitney, THANK YOU. Thank you for the music, the artistry, and the spirit that you shared with the world. We will always love you.

INTRODUCTION
THE GREATEST LOVE OF ALL

"**M**elisma" describes singing a single syllable but moving between different notes while singing it. Done correctly, it requires great skill, and only the most talented performers can manage the feat. Whitney Houston was the master of melismatic singing, with the ability to move seamlessly across her phenomenal vocal range.

But melisma also describes Whitney's life. A life journeying through ups and downs, from the lowest C to the highest G. She navigated forty-eight years of private and public struggles and extraordinary success, filled with acclaim, heartbreak, tragedy, and love. Whitney Houston's life, like her voice, was unique.

Born Whitney Elizabeth Houston in 1963 in Newark, New Jersey, she was raised in a Baptist family with her mother, Cissy, father, John, and brothers Gary and Michael. Music was a part of her world from childhood—Dionne Warwick was a first cousin.

Cissy was a successful singer in her own right, a Grammy Award–winning gospel and soul performer, working with such icons as Elvis Presley and Aretha Franklin. Since the 1960s, Cissy has been a driving force behind the Youth Inspirational Choir at the New Hope Baptist Church in Newark. It was this choir that her daughter performed in and that gave her some of her earliest training, not only in performing to an audience, but also in utilizing her astonishing natural vocal ability.

Whitney Houston had a three-octave range, filled with an immense amount of depth and tone. We can similarly divide her story into three key elements, too: music, family, religion. These cornerstones were the foundation of who she was and intersect constantly throughout her journey and in *I Wanna Dance with Somebody*.

How It All Started

The film began life as a conversation. One half of that conversation was Anthony McCarten, the Oscar-nominated writer and producer whose previous work includes *Bohemian Rhapsody* (2018), *The Two Popes* (2019), *Darkest Hour* (2017), and *The Theory of Everything* (2014). The other half was Clive Davis. Davis is a legend in the music industry, a Rock & Roll Hall of Famer who helped steer the careers of such icons as—to name a few—Bruce Springsteen, Janis Joplin, Aerosmith, Billy Joel, Pink Floyd, Chicago... and Whitney Houston.

"In 2019, a friend invited me to dinner at a New York restaurant and asked if I minded if we were joined by a third," recalls Anthony McCarten. "This person was Clive Davis. Clive had discovered Whitney Houston way back in 1983, when Whitney was singing backup for her mother in a small club in Manhattan. Clive's passion the night we met was that there be a big movie made that would finally celebrate Whitney's musical genius. He'd seen *Bohemian Rhapsody* and seen what a film can do for an artist's currency and standing. So, he invited me to his office at Sony Music the following day. He played songs

Left: Whitney with her mother Cissy (center) and cousin Dionne Warwick (left).

Above: (top) Whitney with Clive Davis in his office at the Arista Studio on the day she signed her recording contract with Arista Records, April 10, 1983; and (bottom) at the taping of "Arista's 25 Years of #1 Hits" on the same day 17 years later, April 10, 2000.

that we both felt no other artist could have sung so well, and I agreed to take on the project. From there, I flew to Atlanta to meet Whitney's brother and sisters-in-law, and then to New York to meet Larry Mestel, whose company, Primary Wave, owns half the Houston estate. From these three meetings, all successful, a partnership was born. Next, I phoned producer and friend Denis O'Sullivan and pitched him the idea of joining me in producing an independently financed film about Whitney featuring her greatest hits. He was game enough not to hang up on me. So that's what we did."

Denis O'Sullivan himself remembers the phone call vividly: "I was in LA and Anthony called me from New York. He just said, 'I think I might have a really big film for us to do.' I went 'Okay…' and then he said one word: 'Whitney.' After their lunch, Clive showed him the video of Whitney performing the American Music Awards medley and explained how no one else on the planet could have done this medley the way she did it. Then Clive told Anthony, 'I think the family is ready to do a film.'"

The Heart of It All: Clive and Pat

The Houston family is represented by Pat Houston, Whitney's sister-in-law and manager. The producers—Anthony McCarten, Denis O'Sullivan, and Jeff Kalligheri—worked closely with Clive Davis, Larry Mestel, and Pat Houston, all of whom are credited as producers on the film. Clive and Pat weighed in on the outlines Anthony wrote, and gave notes on the screenplay drafts. It was a collaboration from Day One, as O'Sullivan explains: "Pat said, the documentary is out there, so there's nothing off-limits. It was one of the first things she said, which I was so impressed by—she said, 'This film is a key piece of Whitney's legacy. We want it to be something that is a celebration within that.' For us, that was really, really great, because it meant that we could go wherever we wanted to go dramatically and not be limited in any way."

Pat and Clive had very personal reasons for wanting to ensure the film was done right. "Clive wasn't thrilled about the 2018 documentary, because there wasn't enough about her music in it," says Pat Houston. "He wanted to do a film and he asked me about producing it with him…. We wanted to deal with the music—how it all started. That's why Clive is so prevalent in the film, from when Whitney was younger, through her story line of music, where she started, when she became an icon, and when it kind of all started to go downhill, including having turbulence within her career and just fighting back to get to where she needed to be. But it was all about the music and where it originated and how she elevated it to become the Whitney Houston we know, through the good and the bad. She started out as a superstar, but she ended up an icon, and that's the story we wanted to tell."

Right: Clive Davis and Pat Houston visit the set.

Writing Whitney's Story: Anthony McCarten

To tell that story, Anthony McCarten was tasked with distilling an entire life into a hundred-plus-page screenplay, a story that does justice to the person at its center, but is also a compelling story onscreen for audiences. The starting point for Anthony, quite simply, was to "Research. Read. Talk to everyone I could. I spoke with everyone I could find, from Clive and the Houston family, down to Whitney's hairstylist, her acting agent, even to her drug therapist. I spoke with Kevin Macdonald, who made the documentary about her. Everyone offered something, and some offered a lot."

McCarten and O'Sullivan had previously worked together on *Bohemian Rhapsody* and, as instructive as that experience had been, they still had to go through the heavy lifting of creating a script with all the hard work that entails.

"It took five iterations of the outline," recalls O'Sullivan. "One of the reasons I love working with Anthony so much, and we work together a lot, is that he's just the most collaborative writer. We started this thing on *Bohemian Rhapsody* where we call the writing process 'getting back in the studio.' It's where we'll kick stuff back and forth, mess around, and play with stuff and see what makes the most sense or what's connecting emotionally. That was the start of the process."

A movie biopic can't just be a run-through of all the key moments of a person's life; a highlight reel is not the same as a story that people are moved by. *I Wanna Dance with Somebody* is about Whitney Houston, but what exactly is it trying to tell us? Much like Whitney rehearsing and rehearsing a song until it was perfect, McCarten and the team continued to craft the script until they'd found the reason for this film to exist.

"Writing is always about rewriting," says McCarten. "You're always looking for more tension, humor, emotion to put into a scene. But the key is honing in on your theme, which is the thing that keeps you from getting lost and going off track. From the outset, I had one word to guide me: Home. In many ways, this was what Whitney was always subconsciously seeking—a home—and I believe she found it at the end, with her daughter, Bobbi Kristina. If there is a single word that sums up this movie for me, it's that word."

Denis O'Sullivan confirms this, after Pat Houston shared with him Whitney's own feelings about Bobbi Kristina; "Whitney had said Bobbi Kristina was the only person who'd purely loved her for who she was. When you have a gift, a purpose, such as to share your voice with the world, how do you also find a home for yourself? I think that she went through iterations of it and then finally found it with her daughter."

Above: Anthony McCarten discusses a scene with director Kasi Lemmons.

Right: Whitney with her daughter Bobbi Kristina at the Clive Davis Pre-Grammy Awards party, February 12, 2011.

"Whitney had said Bobbi Kristina was the only person who'd purely loved her for who she was. When you have a gift, a purpose, such as to share your voice with the world, how do you also find a home for yourself? I think that she went through iterations of it and then finally found it with her daughter." –Pat Houston

Putting It All Together: The Producers

Whitney Houston's music is filled with emotion. She feels and expresses her songs with a rare depth and honesty. This speaks to her gospel background, where so much love and praise and meaning is told through song. Whitney passed away in 2012; today, there is a sense that, with some time having elapsed, her true legacy and impact is only just being felt.

"Being as close as I was to her for many years, watching her onstage," reminisces Pat Houston, "she was absolutely flawless. When you have the opportunity on tour to be up close and personal and be around such an icon and such a talent, now seeing it reenacted, it's beautiful. It's like you're hearing her voice all over again, and you know why you fell in love with her from the very beginning. It was bittersweet for me."

"Our goal was to create a celebration of a life cut short," says O'Sullivan. "To understand how lucky we were to have her on the planet at all."

The ambition was to make a big movie, the sort of movie that typically gets produced through traditional Hollywood studios. But the producers, Jeff Kalligheri in particular, steered the ship in a different direction. Kalligheri and O'Sullivan had been friends for 17 years and were looking to formally start a company together. They decided to start with something big.

"Denis delivered *Bohemian Rhapsody* then left his former company. He is a true creative genius and had received a bunch of offers but he told me he wanted to work with me so I jumped at the chance and Compelling Pictures was born. We already had a development fund and multiple projects in the works from my preexisting investor Dennis Casali, which I moved over to Compelling. Then Denis mentioned to me—having already spoken with Anthony—that we might get the Whitney Houston movie. I was like . . . really? As a new company it was a massive undertaking for us. It was like walking a tightrope. One of the first people we spoke to was Larry Mestel, whose company Primary Wave owns half the Houston estate, who became one of the originating producers on the film. Denis met with him and called me afterward and he said, 'Larry asked if we could cofinance this movie—if we had the ability to do that.' I told Denis no; we would fully finance it. That was the package we put together: With the family and Primary Wave officially involved as producers, Anthony writing it, and Compelling Pictures fully funding it. That way we would be a part of the upside—all of the artists get a piece—and also retain creative control. Unlike one of those films where they relegate the family or the estate to being a passive participant, this was the opposite of that. We always felt that Pat and Clive and Larry were giving us an opportunity to be part of their team, and we were going to make them proud and do it right. We wanted to make sure they would actually make money in the process and share in the success that could come. Pat, Clive, and Larry were on board, with Anthony and Denis heading up the creative side. It was my job to finance the movie and package it in the best way we could. I negotiated every single talent deal, every single contract. Normally our lawyer Evan Krauss would do it, but this was such a big movie for us that I wanted to be a

Left: Producers Pat Houston (center) and Lawrence Mestel (*right*) visit Naomi Ackie (Whitney) and Nafessa Williams (Robyn) during the filming of the Super Bowl scene.

Above: Producers Denis O'Sullivan (*top*) and Jeff Kalligheri (*bottom*) shooting at Gillette Stadium in Foxborough, Massachussetts.

> "The one we felt had the most passion for the project, hands down, was Sony. Its theatrical support for films is super important to us. We decided to partner with Sony right around the time a lot of big studios were dumping major movies on streaming, and Sony was the only company that didn't have a streamer." —Jeff Kalligheri

part of every single process. My name is on each contract. I mean, how often do you get to make the Whitney Houston movie?

"The pieces were all coming together. The first announcement goes out. It was the fastest I'd ever seen a project go from idea to script to director attachment to announcement. Then the whole plan that we'd started with was we're going to package it and finance it ourselves and go out to the town to get worldwide distribution—to create a bidding war, essentially. When the package went out a ton of people bid on it and it came down to two studios. The one that we felt had the most passion for the project, hands down, was Sony. Their theatrical support for films is super important for us. We decided to partner with them right around the time a lot of the big studios were dumping major movies on streaming and Sony was the only company that didn't have a streamer. One of the aims of our company, Compelling Pictures, is to keep the theatrical experience alive."

Another team that provided key support for the picture was Black Label Media, a production company whose enviable track record includes *Sicario* (2015) and *La La Land* (2016). Molly Smith, Trent Luckinbill, and Thad Luckinbill are producers on the movie as part of Black Label Media. They were already aware of the project when Compelling Pictures reached out to them about partnering on the film, as Smith explains: "We took a look at everything and obviously spoke to Denis and Jeff and Anthony and loved the project. It was sort of fast and furious because it was already a moving train—they were prepping in Boston at that point. I will say the only other film we sort of got involved in when it was already shooting was *La La Land*, so we felt like it was a sign, since it was a project we already loved. We happily jumped on board. I've always been a huge Whitney fan, and I think what spoke to us about this film in particular was how there have been documentaries and there have been many specials on Whitney, but there's never been anything that gave you a really intimate look at Whitney the person and her rise to fame; this complicated life she led, becoming one of the biggest global superstars of all time. What we loved as well about what they're doing with the movie is that while Whitney, of course, had a lot of tragedy and struggles in her life, the movie really celebrates her."

The film was edging closer and closer to being a reality, and, at a certain point, everyone realized it was a reality—*I Wanna Dance with Somebody* was happening. "There's a great Lorne Michaels quote," says O'Sullivan. "*Saturday Night Live* doesn't go on because it's ready, it goes on because it's Saturday at 11:30. I feel there's an element of that with movies, where you can always keep adding prep weeks, or whatever, but there's a point where you just have to go."

It had taken on a life of its own, but two key pieces were still missing: a director and, of course, a Whitney.

Right: On set with cast and crew *(l-r)* Screenwriter Anthony McCarten, Naomi Ackie (Whitney), director Kasi Lemmons, Nafessa Williams (Robyn), producer Matt Jackson, executive producer Seth Spector, producer Jeff Kalligheri, and executive producer Josh Crook.

"This film is a key piece of Whitney's legacy. We want it to be something that is a celebration within that. For us, that was really, really great, because it meant that we could go wherever we wanted to go dramatically and not be limited in any way."—Denis O'Sullivan

Getting Direction: Kasi Lemmons

"Kasi was actually my first choice for director," says Pat Houston. "She just wasn't available when we initiated the film. But she was always my first choice."

Kasi Lemmons is a director, screenwriter, and actor. Early recognition came via starring roles in films such as *School Daze* (1988), *Silence of the Lambs* (1991), and *Candyman* (1992), before transitioning to filmmaking with *Eve's Bayou* (1997), *Dr. Hugo* (1996), and, more recently, *Harriet* (2019)—the historical biopic focused on Harriet Tubman, which received critical acclaim and a multitude of award nominations. Lemmons was a perfect fit to transfer Whitney's story to screen. The only problem was, she couldn't do it.

"Kasi is not doing this film because she has some free time on her hands," confirms O'Sullivan. "She didn't want to do the film because she had so much else on. When we started talking to Kasi and her agent, Frank Wuliger, they asked if we could push everything from September 2021 to January 2022. We had all the crew and everything lined up and Jeff and I said, "no, not really. We've got to do it this year." I spent a weekend doing a calendar to accommodate for Kasi's other work commitments, including mounting an opera at the Metropolitan Opera House at Lincoln Center [in New York City]. I did five iterations and kept sending them to Frank. Then I remember seeing an email from Kasi to Frank that Frank had forwarded to Jeff, and she said in her message, Frank, I can see they're really trying to make this work. You know, let's figure it out."

Figure it out they did, and Kasi Lemmons joined the production seven weeks before shooting commenced. There was no time to waste, but, it speaks to Lemmons's diligence that she made the time to go through every aspect of the film, giving specific attention to the cornerstone of the project: the script.

Kasi Lemmons directing a scene on the beach *(left)* and taking a break on the set of Sweetwater's *(above)*.

"The very first thing I did was meet with all the departments, to see where they were and if it was a relationship that was going to work for me, honestly," explains Lemmons. "I really wanted to work with Anthony on the script, and really crystallize what he was trying to say and what I wanted to say. Anthony was amazing to work with. He's just very collaborative and willing to keep going at it. It was about making it leaner and bringing things into focus: What were the main themes? It's a biographical movie, but it's still a movie, so what are the main themes? Just trying to be as close to our character as we

"To me, there was a very important story about an artist and her instrument. That was very pertinent to Whitney. People I talked to…said that once her voice was gone, that really was it…Of course, she participated in the destruction of it. But at the same time, it kind of moved me on a big cosmic level."—Kasi Lemmons

Right: Kasi working with Naomi on the set of the music video "Run to You."

Far right: The "Run to You" set.

could, as well as thinning out the script a bit, then deciding which parts were the most urgent and essential."

Aside from her experience and technical ability and attitude, what Lemmons brought to the project was an extraordinary level of empathy and humanity. Whitney's voice was transcendent, and everyone involved in the film, including Lemmons, was reaching for that same beauty.

"To me, there was a very important story about an artist and her instrument," says Lemmons. "That was very pertinent to Whitney, because the people I talked to or read said that once her voice was gone, that really was it. They equated her voice with her demise—direct, indirect, and metaphorical. I thought that was interesting, and it became something I was quite moved by. What happens when you have a God-given gift, and you kind of take it for granted? Whitney loved to sing, and she had such amazing range and such an amazing gift. And yet it faded. It left her and it left her pretty quickly; she was probably struggling by the late nineties. It was a temporary God-given gift. Of course, she participated in the destruction of it. But at the same time, it kind of moved me on a big cosmic level."

Pat Houston was correct in her prediction: Kasi Lemmons was the right person for the job. As with all the key players on the film, the ability to do the work melded with a passion to do it right. "I just felt that she could tell Whitney's story," confirms Houston. "It's her integrity, understanding the story line, understanding Whitney's life. She was very transparent, and if there was something on set that I thought wasn't authentic, she changed it without any resistance. She was the consummate professional, and she listened. She listened to understand and not to react. And I love that about her."

If the movie can be compared to a concert, at this point the orchestra was assembled and tuned up, the conductor was in position, the stage was set, the spotlight was on, and now everyone was just waiting for the leading lady.

CHAPTER 1

SAVING ALL MY LOVE FOR YOU
FINDING WHITNEY

> " Pat Houston said, 'I have to act as though Whitney is gonna be sitting beside me watching this movie and if she would be pissed off that something's completely false, or if we pulled punches on something when we should have gone harder.' She had to honor what Whitney would think of this movie. "
>
> —Denis O'Sullivan

At the heart of this project is Whitney Houston herself. She is recognized the world over and held dearly in the hearts of devoted fans, and everyone on the film understood from the outset that there will never be another Whitney. It would be a fool's errand to attempt to mirror her and trick audiences into thinking it is the one and only Whitney on-screen. What they needed was someone who could embody the legend and express her story in the most honest and empathetic way.

"Pat Houston once said something to me that I thought was really interesting," recalls Denis O'Sullivan. "She said, 'I have to act as though Whitney is gonna be sitting beside me watching this movie and if she would be pissed off that something's completely false, or if we pulled punches on something when we should have gone harder.' She explained how they were so close, and she had to honor what Whitney would think of this movie."

The movie could not be afraid to go to some difficult places. Accordingly, they needed an actor who wouldn't be afraid to go there with it. The pressure was on—and the hunt for the right actor began.

"It was a long process," continues O'Sullivan, explaining how the producers and casting director, Kim Coleman, conducted their search. "Bear in mind, this is in the middle of the pandemic. We're doing all these auditions on Zoom and it's different from being in the room and really getting to know someone. We had open auditions at churches and drama schools and music schools. We were really casting a wide net to see if we could just find Whitney. Kim and Anna [McCarthy]—who works with her—were sifting through all these tapes and sending the best of the best to us. And I remember watching Naomi's first audition."

Auditioning Naomi

Naomi Ackie is a London-born actor, perhaps most familiar to audiences from her work in the award-winning TV series *The End of the F****g World* and the blockbuster *Star Wars: The Rise of Skywalker* (2019). *I Wanna Dance with Somebody* was brought to her by her agents and it was a step-by-step process.

"Initially, I was like, this is absolutely insane," remembers Ackie. "I'll give it a go, but I really don't think I'm going to get that far through the auditions for a number of reasons. I had a meeting with the director and with Denis. And whenever the next round of auditions would come through, it just seemed like whatever I was doing, I was doing it right—but I didn't know what it was and I couldn't quite figure it out. I was just surprised every time they asked me to come back. Then I remember being on set on a different film and getting a call from my agent saying, 'They want to do a camera test with you on Halloween. They've been flying everyone over.' I've never been involved with a job where

Previous page: Naomi Ackie before becoming Whitney, at the premiere of *Star Wars: The Rise of Skywalker* in London.

Right: Naomi as a young Whitney Houston, getting ready for her first recording session.

> "When you are taking on the body language and characteristics of somebody that already exists, it is a huge negotiation between what is known about that person and what isn't known about that person." —Polly Bennett

Above: Naomi's audition setting eerily looked like the now-iconic "I Will Always Love You" video, which Naomi would ultimately do in the movie.

people fly to see people. So, I was like, oh, that's a big deal. On Halloween they dress me up as close as they could to Whitney so I could do some songs and some scenes. By the end, when I left, I was thinking I don't know what it means, but it felt good in the moment and what will be will be."

Denis O'Sullivan has a different perspective on the final audition. "It's Halloween 2020. Anthony and I are in the car on the way to the camera test and he asks, 'What if it doesn't work? I believe it will, but what if it doesn't?' I said that when she steps in front of the camera, you and I will look at each other and we will acknowledge that to ourselves and we won't talk about it until we get to the end of the day, and then we'll regroup and figure it out. So, we arrive and it takes some time for her to get made up and all that. I'm standing with him on the small soundstage and it's quite dark, with just some top-lighting, so it looked a little bit like the 'I Will Always Love You' video. Anthony and I are standing there, and Naomi brushes past us in the dark about ten feet away, so we really can't see her. Then she comes into the light in front of the camera. We're at the monitors, and I just remember he grabbed my arm. He just looked at me and smiled as soon as she stepped in front of the camera. We both felt, Okay, this is the person."

Throughout the audition process, Naomi received some big endorsements, says O'Sullivan. "I showed her audition tape to my friends from *Bohemian Rhapsody*—Rami Malik, Lucy Boynton, Gwilym Lee, Ben Hardy, and Joe Mazzello. I showed them five auditions and I didn't editorialize. All of them said she's just stunning. She's just incredible. We all had the same reaction.

"Clive Davis said she has that sparkle in her eye."

As for the moment Naomi found out she got the part? "I sat on the floor with my agents. We drank a bottle of champagne and just freaked out."

Capturing Whitney

After the hard work of auditions and tests came the real hard work: finding a way to capture and express Whitney truthfully on-screen. Ackie had to do justice to the words on the page by Anthony McCarten, but also to this global icon, knowing that every fan who watches the film will be evaluating her performance. To help in her mission, Naomi was partnered with renowned movement coach Polly Bennett. Bennett had also worked with Rami Malek on *Bohemian Rhapsody* and Austin Butler on *Elvis* (2022). The very philosophy of bringing a real-life character to life on film was discussed at the start, and together they established that it is not about mimicry. An impersonation of Whitney Houston would not allow Naomi Ackie to express the inner life of the singer or enable her to do anything other than act out preplanned moves.

"When you are taking on the body language and characteristics of somebody that already exists, it is a huge negotiation between what is known about that person and what isn't known about that person," explains Bennett. "Naomi and I cross-sectioned all the stuff that we knew, or thought we knew, and tried to work out the things that we didn't know. Because that's where the character stuff comes in, and that's the most important bit for an actor. You're not ever going: 'We're gonna watch this footage and replicate this.' Anyone could do that. Anyone could sit in front of the screen and tirelessly cover it. I'm interested in finding out for an actor or discovering with an actor why a person does the

Above: Working with renowned movement coach Polly Bennett to get Whitney's performance gestures just right. Bennett: *"[Movement coaching] goes beyond choreography and stage performances. It is about trying to find the reason why that person needs to go on stage. The majority of our first bits of work were about finding what is in her, why she has to sing."*

Overleaf: Choreographer James Alsop *(right)* giving pointers on Whitney's singing style, as director Kasi Lemmons (center) looks on. Alsop: *"Whitney carried herself in a way that really and truly only focused on her voice and that permeated her performances, from choreography to costuming to hair, to makeup–everything. I absolutely loved that about her and I loved bringing that kind of movement because it's just so joyous."*

Above: Capturing Whitney's off-stage body language was just as important as her onstage performance style work. Polly (left) and Naomi worked tirelessly to get everything just right. Bennett: *"We're not just looking at a section of a person's life, we are spanning the entire person's life. So what are the qualities that somebody holds on to all the way through and what are the things that they let go of as they age?"*

Opposite: Naomi discussing a key moment in the concert montage with Kasi and Clarke Peters (John Houston).

movements that they do and why people act the way that they do. Our first meeting was going right back to who Whitney was, how she grew up—the components of her existence, which is her family, her faith, her relationships with her brothers, her relationships with each of her parents, the relationship with the church, her relationship to the streets, the relationships to being from where she's from. We looked at photographs of when she was a kid, trying to find a semblance of the body language and the physicality that we understand her to have later on."

Polly Bennett may be credited as "Movement Coach" but the work she and Naomi conducted went right to the psychology of Whitney. They wanted to understand why Whitney Houston felt the need to sing. What drove her to perform? This speaks to the oldest adage about acting—that a character must have motivation. By unlocking Whitney's needs and wants, Naomi was able to react how Whitney would. She was not attempting to copy Whitney; she was trying to summon Houston's very real desires, drives, and tension. It's not so much "How did Whitney react in that moment?" but more "How would Whitney react in this moment?"

"What I started to experience during the whole filming process," says Ackie, "was that the work we had done started to subconsciously feed into performance work. We just had Whitney, you know, walking the world. You really stop separating performance -person-performance-person and you meld them together. Certain tics that she might have, that I've spotted in interviews, would suddenly find themselves in performances and sometimes the way that she would walk in performances would change the energy

I would feel in different scenes. I tried to make it as fluid as possible."

What Naomi had on her side was time. She was cast following the Halloween 2020 audition and shooting did not begin until September 2021. This gave Naomi the opportunity to hone her approach and really have Whitney's physicality become second nature. Ackie likens it to muscle memory and how much faster and more adept you get at an exercise because you're so familiar with it. Together, Polly and Naomi named all of Whitney's performances with titles (such as "Princess in a Tracksuit") that acted as a shorthand for the physicality and psychology of those performances. "I've still got the video of Polly recording me and then shouting out a movement and me being able to do it," says Ackie. "They are part of Whitney's repertoire of movements to communicate a song. Your body starts to connect with the words, but it also connects with an emotion and an energy."

Houston was not the type of performer who learned complicated dance routines. As a result, casual viewers may struggle to identify Whitney's onstage persona. When she started the project, people asked Polly exactly what she would be working on, because Whitney "doesn't do very much"—a statement Bennett vehemently opposes. "Yes, she does! She does so much. She's from the gospel church, so in her is gospel breathing, and that control or how she uses her arms to navigate and conduct the band, particularly when she gets older. She's conducting the bands and they are often slightly behind her, with her charging ahead. A hand movement from Whitney that looks simple isn't—it's loaded with the history of everything she is.... She is carrying with her the wealth of her experience. That's what Naomi's challenge was: to communicate the physicality of someone who has only ever sung."

"Often your instinct is 'I'm older so I must play older,'" But sometimes it's actually the fight to still be young. So, where the natural bounciness of a nineteen-year-old is just there, in middle age that bounciness is maybe a bit more conscious. It's not the sadness of not having the same singing voice, but it's the fight to get the voice back."–Naomi Ackie

Above: A struggling Whitney fighting to get the voice back.

Opposite: Thirty years in two hours: Going from bouncing adolescence to middle-age was not just about hair and makeup. Charlese Antoinette Jones: *"People forget how iconic she was, and just how original and how powerful her voice was because there's so many things later in her life that overshadow how important she is."*

Learning How to Age

The film doesn't give simply a snapshot of Whitney's life; this *is* Whitney's life. We see her from her adolescence to her death at forty-eight. The film tracks thirty years of her life and career, including the emotional peaks and troughs. So much can be achieved through hair, makeup, and costuming, but the role required Naomi to switch from one day to the next playing Whitney at different ages. How she achieved this was not by analyzing how a forty-year-old person talks and moves, but how Whitney at forty talked and moved.

"Often your instinct is 'I'm older so I must play older,'" says Ackie. "But sometimes it's actually the fight to still be young. So, where the natural bounciness of a nineteen-year-old is just there, in middle age that bounciness is maybe a bit more conscious. It's not the sadness of not having the same singing voice, but it's the fight to get the voice back. The mental state is: 'I'm okay, I'm gonna get through this, or, perhaps, I don't know what's wrong. Everyone is looking at me like something's wrong and everything is fine.' In terms of age and performing the areas of her life that were more difficult, for me it was a kind of about playing the opposites and not playing the 'tragedy,' because at those points in the story, no one knows. The dramatic irony is that we know what happens to Whitney, sadly, but she doesn't know. It helped me to play it a bit more truthfully. When I go through really hard times, I don't tend to know I've gone through a really hard time until I've looked back on it."

What Is Regal?

The pressure to pull the role off was intense, as everyone has their own idea of who Whitney was and how she should be portrayed, something they encountered even while filming. It is not possible to please everyone, as Bennett explains:

"If Naomi is given a note, which is 'be more regal,' everyone's concept of what regality is is different. My job is to try and turn that into a physical, practical, playable thing so that Naomi isn't getting on set and one person is saying Whitney's regal, another person is saying her back should be straight, etc. Naomi would be trying to honor all of these things, but with no physical foundation."

Naomi Ackie elaborates on this point: "I totally see from a costuming point of view how you can create a regal form. When it comes to acting, it's more: What is the attitude about regality? How do you feel about being regal? Are you putting it on? Are you pretending? Is it something you're trying to fight? Do you use it as a weapon sometimes? It's taking all those kinds of notes about Whitney and other people's perceptions of her and then considering, How would she feel about those perceptions? And when would she use those perceptions to get what she wants or to hide away or to deflect?"

The Separation of Self

Much has been written about storied actors losing themselves in a role, and, while this makes for easy headlines, it wasn't the case for Naomi, with Polly advising her to take a more realistic approach.

"Where I was absorbing so much of Whitney for about a year and a half, my movements and Whitney's movements started to meld together. Even if I wasn't consciously acting like Whitney, sometimes I would clock myself doing a nod or a mannerism like her. It was like practicing without practicing. When I started this project, I decided, out of fear, really, that as soon as I touched foot in America, I would only talk in an American accent. My idea was that I'm literally just gonna be like Whitney Houston at 40 every day, and then on set I'll be able to take it up to 150percent. It was Polly who said, 'I don't think that's a good idea, because you need to have a separation of self.' That was one of the pearls that I still hold dear. It wasn't about necessarily which movements were mine and which were Whitney's; it was more about how to separate and keep from delving into somebody else's world that isn't yours. I'm an actor. I pretend. I'm not going around actually thinking that I'm Whitney Houston."

The filmmakers had their Whitney. Now they just needed to cast everyone else.

Right: Naomi dropping the Whitney mask and letting her own personality shine through between takes.

CHAPTER 2

I WANNA DANCE WITH SOMEBODY

THE SUPPORTING CHARACTERS

66 The challenge is always the same when you attempt projects that are rooted in the life of someone so famous and beloved: You have to honor the facts as we know them, but then also offer something new and fresh that makes the experience worth the price of admission. 99
—Anthony McCarten

CLIVE DAVIS
PORTRAYED BY STANLEY TUCCI

Music industry giant Clive Davis first laid eyes—and ears—on Whitney Houston in 1983. She performed on stage at Sweetwater's in New York City, singing "The Greatest Love of All." It is a moment immortalized in *I Wanna Dance with Somebody*, with Davis reflecting that, "I may have just heard the greatest voice of her generation." In the film, as in real life, a partnership, a friendship, a bond was formed between Clive and Whitney, one that would remain unbroken throughout her career.

Clive Davis was at her side for every one of her hits, popping a bottle of Dom Pérignon with her for each number-one record. Together, they knew better than anyone which songs were right for Whitney—not only which ones best suited her voice, but also those that spoke to her emotionally. They understood one another, and that shows not only in terms of their commercial success, but also in the longevity of their relationship.

"The film idea actually originated with Clive Davis," confirms Pat Houston. "Clive and I have had a very close relationship for many, many, many years. And, of course, you can't mention one name without the other when you're talking about Clive or when you're talking about Whitney. I always tell people that if you have one loyal friend, it's better than having ten thousand relatives, and Clive was that one loyal friend."

Opposite: Stanley Tucci as Clive Davis, in his booth at Sweetwater's waiting to hear if this new Houston girl is everything she's cracked up to be.

Below: (left) Whitney signing her contract with Clive Davis at his office on April 10, 1983, and *(right)* Stanley and Naomi re-creating that moment.

> "There's a tremendous chemistry between Stanley and Naomi, and a real warmth and love and humor, even beyond what's on the page. I find it quite heartbreaking when we get to the end of the film and understand that their playfulness has ceased to be."—Denis O'Sullivan

This spread: At every stage of her life and career, Whitney's talks with Clive were her touchstone; they became the through-line for the entire film. Pat Houston: *"Stanley Tucci was a no brainer. We could not do it without him. Casting Stanley Tucci was the easiest of them all."*

Indeed, no matter what was going on in her personal life, working with Clive created a safe space for Whitney. It was in these moments that they were able to indulge in and celebrate their greatest passion: music.

"I've worked on music film biopics," states Denis O'Sullivan, "and having the 'record company guy' be a true friend and ally, someone who deeply loves her and is there for her, having some of the really difficult conversations—that's unusual. I don't know that I've seen that in music biopics because usually the record guys can be portrayed as naysayers, arguing the song is too long, or whatever. So, to see someone from the start of her career through to the end and outliving the artist even and having this gorgeous, tender relationship, I think that's unique."

Perhaps the most well-known relationship in Whitney's life was her marriage to Bobby Brown, and, of course, that is covered in the movie. But the Whitney-Clive friendship is a thread that runs through the film and actually signifies the longest meaningful connection she had outside of family. The movie takes us into Clive's office at key beats in her career, but also for some quieter moments.

"I love all the scenes that relate to Whitney and Clive," says Pat Houston. "I love those scenes with that relationship because I know how honest and pure and truthful it was. That relationship was just what it was, no hidden agendas. They were very transparent with one another. And I love seeing them interact on- screen, just as I did when she was here."

It was a special connection, and to conjure it on-screen they needed a special actor, which they found in Stanley Tucci.

A legendary and prolific character actor, Tucci has worked with everyone from Steven Spielberg and Sam Mendes to Peter Jackson and John Huston. He is Oscar-nominated, BAFTA-nominated, Grammy-nominated, Tony-nominated, and the winner of four Emmy awards. His name is a mark of quality, and when it came to portraying Clive Davis, it was the only one on the list.

"He's the person Clive wanted from the very beginning," confirms O'Sullivan. "Making a movie during COVID, everyone had so many projects going, so we tried to go to Stanley early on and he was doing a show and then we pushed things back, then he got into another movie…. For it all to line up eventually and to have Stanley for three weeks to shoot was a miracle, an absolute miracle.

"There's a tremendous chemistry between Stanley and Naomi and a real warmth and love and humor, even beyond what's on the page. I find it quite heartbreaking when we get to the end of the film and understand that their playfulness has ceased to be."

"It's a fascinating relationship," says Kasi Lemmons, "because it went from the beginning right to the end. I think he loved her. There's no question. And it was a real friendship, yet he positioned himself as being somebody who is very professional and all about the work, but in working so closely, they became like family. I think it's a really important relationship. And, of course, I love Stanley. Those scenes are great. They found an amazing, lived-in relationship, which is a wonderful thing between actors. It's that magic thing, that chemistry when you get really good actors working together. It's like they've been together forever. It was really exciting to work with them."

ROBYN CRAWFORD
PORTRAYED BY NAFESSA WILLIAMS

Robyn Crawford met Whitney when they were teenagers. Crucially, they were best friends before Whitney became a worldwide superstar, and Robyn therefore became a trusted ally.

In order to create their Robyn for *I Wanna Dance with Somebody*, Nafessa Williams (of TV's *Black Lightning* and *Twin Peaks: The Return* among others) was cast—although that wasn't the part she originally read for.

"I initially auditioned for Whitney in 2020, then it later came back around for me to audition for Robyn. I thought this was a really cool opportunity to play somebody who not a lot of people know a lot about. I sent a tape in first. I guess it went well because then I got a call back to read with Naomi. I could feel it went well . . . [we had] so much chemistry together. Naomi had already been booked as Whitney and I could feel her cheering me on. I could see that Kasi was happy as well. I felt really good about it. Afterward, I just thought, 'I'm expecting to hear from them next week'. You know when you know. And I did get the call . . . and a couple of weeks later I was in Boston filming."

Any portrayal of a real-life person requires research. While Nafessa did a deep dive into who Robyn Crawford was and is, she was also able to draw on her own experiences and memories. "I grew up in the '90s, so this was something I knew a lot about. We're also the same sign–Sagittarius. There's

Left: Nafessa Williams as Robyn Crawford.

Below: Nafessa and Naomi in two scenes from the early days of Whitney's and Robyn's friendship.

"I remember Pat being on set when we were shooting a scene where Whitney and Robyn have a fight. They're talking about their relationship, and I just remember Pat sitting there looking at me and after the take saying, 'This is amazing. This is beautiful.'"—Denis O'Sullivan

Above: Naomi and Nafessa sharing a lighthearted moment on set.

Opposite: Whitney gathering strength and courage from Robyn before the filming of the "How Will I Know" video.

a lot of who I am that I saw in her and I brought that to the character—very charming, very fun, very loyal. Die-hard loyalty."

Nafessa also immersed herself in the time period, looking at the fashions, the hairstyles, watching the movies, creating a feeling of the era. "I made a Robyn playlist that I would listen to every morning before I would go to work and while I was on set. 'Rock Steady' was my favorite. A lot of Babyface, obviously a lot of Whitney, a lot of Teddy Pendergrass, 'Freaks Come Out at Night' by Whodini, 'Say it Loud—I'm Black and I'm Proud' by James Brown. Those are just some of the songs I used to get me in the mode of Robyn.

"There's a process I have as an actor. Once you get into hair and makeup and you really get into the vibe of the scene there's a natural buildup. Being there filming for three months I was pretty much already in the zone of who she is, so I tried to stay in that pocket as best as possible. Obviously, it's turned up when I'm on set. I like to do very thorough, deep character work that'll carry me through filming. . . . Playing Robyn at different ages was a challenge. You have more energy in your younger years. She walks a certain way at eighteen. She holds her posture differently in her thirties and forties. It's about making sure I'm authentic to that era. Kasi always did a good job of helping us remember where we were."

Pat Houston (above, with Nafessa) was on hand to advise on Robyn's key personality traits, so that Nafessa's portrayal, through all of the trials and tribulations of Robyn's and Whitney's relationship, was as truthful as possible.

Overleaf: Whitney (Naomi) and Robyn (Nafessa) in a private moment on the set of the music video for "How Will I Know."

"One thing that Kasi said to me was when I was wondering if I should meet Robyn. As an artist you're trying to soak up as much knowledge as you can. Kasi said, 'I don't think you need to. You have everything that you need in you to do this character.' With the trust in myself and then her reassuring that . . . she allowed me to be safe and gave us liberty to be ourselves and put who we are into the characters. That was a note that carried me through the film."

The key periods from Robyn and Whitney's lives are living memory for many people. Nafessa Williams grew up during these times and stepping back into them now was akin to something like time travel. "It was very surreal. I always wanted to be an adult in the '90s, so I was like, 'I'm able to do this!' I'm able to wear the heavy, oversized leather jackets! I remember being a kid and watching the Super Bowl and the Soul Train Awards and seeing them in the audience . . . I would be on set as Robyn, but I would also be on set as a fan watching Naomi because I'm such a fan of Whitney. I would just watch in awe and have chills. It brought me to tears a couple of times."

As well as hair and makeup transforming the long-haired Nafessa to resemble the short-haired Robyn, Pat Houston was also on-hand to advise on key personality traits.

"I made a point about Whitney and Robyn. I said Robyn was very cool and laid back. She wasn't giddy in public with Whitney because she wasn't. She was very professional, and there was no giddiness or playing around and goofing off. That wasn't Robyn's personality when she was working. And they got it. But that stood out a great deal. I just wanted everyone to be portrayed as close to their personality as could be."

The advice was taken on board, with the film constantly striving for historical and emotional truth. "I remember Pat being on set when we were shooting a scene where Whitney and Robyn have a fight," recalls producer Denis O'Sullivan. "They're talking about their relationship, and I just remember Pat sitting there looking at me and, after the take saying, `This is amazing. This is beautiful.'"

BOBBY BROWN
PORTRAYED BY ASHTON SANDERS

Ashton Sanders capturing every aspect of Bobby Brown, from bad-boy musician and elated boyfriend to frustrated–and frustrating–husband. Audiences will see Bobby and Whitney's relationship like never before.

When a movie biopic is released there is a certain "box-checking" exercise that happens with some critics and audiences, where the viewer is simply waiting to see what they believe they already know played out on the screen. The film, in effect, becomes a "greatest hits" record. With regard to the relationship between Whitney Houston and Bobby Brown, everyone already thinks they know the story. For the filmmakers, however, it wasn't so much about what was left to tell, but how to tell it. As Anthony McCarten explains, "The challenge is always the same when you attempt projects that are rooted in the life of someone so famous and beloved: You have to honor the facts as we know them, but then also offer something new and fresh that makes the experience worth the price of admission."

Denis O'Sullivan specifically addresses Bobby's role not only in the film but also in Whitney's life—informed by all the exhaustive research they undertook for the movie. "With Bobby, I think the script gives him a more nuanced portrayal than the media has. By Whitney's own admission, she was into drugs and the like before she ever met Bobby, but I think a lot of people have this perception that he took her down this bad path. They were not healthy for each other at all, and there's a lot of shit that he did that is reprehensible, I would say, but the notion that she was pure, and then he took her down this road is just fundamentally not true."

I think that by trying to get next to their love and their sexual attraction, I was attempting to get across what appealed to them about each other, and some of that toxicity, too." —Kasi Lemmons

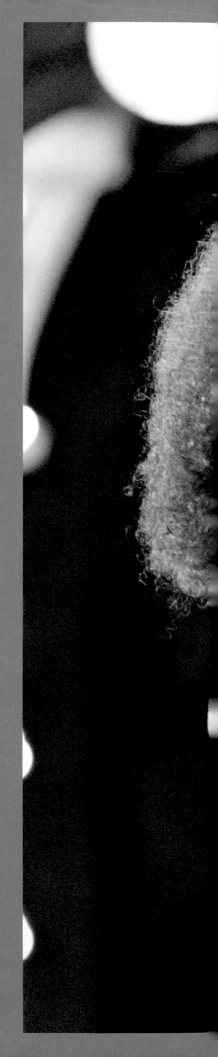

Bobby is not the devil on Whitney's shoulder, nor is he an angel. What the film strives to show is that he is and was multiple things all at the same time: a highly successful, platinum-selling recording artist; an important pop culture figure in 1980s music; troubled; handsome; a father; a husband; a cheater. He was human.

Brown is played by Ashton Sanders, who is perhaps best known for his role in 2016's *Moonlight*. Paired with Naomi Ackie, Sanders has to show the audience what really happened in Whitney and Bobby's tempestuous marriage, from their first meeting to their breakup.

"They lived in public to a large extent, with the reality show and everything, so I didn't want to recap any of that," says Kasi Lemmons. "I just wanted to get to the sense of their playfulness, and what might have been appealing about it to her. And then a hint of the toxicity of it; how these two people are not good for each other, and it starts to go south pretty quickly. But there is a reason that they stayed together so long, and I think that it had to do with a lot of things. I think it had to do with where her head was at the time about the image she was presenting and the response that she was getting, some of the pushback from the Black audience and all of that. I think she felt she could be herself with Bobby. In the movie, he promises her, 'You can be yourself with me, you don't have to be Whitney Houston for a second.' I think that was very appealing. I think that by trying to get next to their love and their sexual attraction, I was attempting to get across what appealed to them about each other, and some of that toxicity, too."

We first meet Brown, as Whitney does, at the Soul Train Music Awards, which was at the tail end of the 1980s, but still gave Charlese Antoinette Jones, the costumer, a chance to dive into the fashions of the era, especially via Bobby's styling.

"There's an amazing jeweler I work with a lot in New York, and we re-created this crown chain that Bobby wears a lot during the '80s, and a couple of other chains he wears. We sent photos, did sketches and the renderings, and made them because I felt that was important. My research showed he wore it a lot. We finally found a color photo of it that we zoomed in on and realized that each stone in the crown was a different color. Very cool. A lot of the details I really liked I honed in on it because I wanted it to match his taste. Even if his outfits

Bobby Brown was the epitome of late-1980s rapper fashion, down to his jewel-encrusted crown necklace that costumer Charlese Antoinette Jones had re-created for the film.

in scenes weren't necessarily the same as things I'd seen him in during my research, I just wanted the feeling to be there. There was one image of him in a long, exaggerated, black, moto-style trench coat—moto, but it was long. I had that re-created, and we have him in that for one of the scenes where he is coming home to the mansion drunk or whatever. He was out partying."

For his part, Sanders was happy to inhabit the role fully, including Bobby's trademark hairstyle, as hairstylist Brian Badie explains. "The Bobby Brown gumby was definitely a moment I was looking forward to. That hairstyle was kind of famous back then. Re-creating that on Ashton was definitely a significant moment in my career. I used the topper, which is like a toupee, and I just attached it to Ashton's hair, but then I kind of built hair around it and then cut it on a diagonal thirty-five-degree angle. Ashton really liked it. He definitely has an eye for detail. You can tell he knew what he wanted to make this character come to life, so I was proud that I made him feel comfortable enough to help with his process. I feel like if the hair hadn't been right, it would have been a whole other story. What actor's gonna feel comfortable if the hair isn't right—or makeup, or costume, you know? We all have to be there to make them feel comfortable and secure when they go on set, so they feel the character."

CISSY HOUSTON
PORTRAYED BY TAMARA TUNIE

For all the natural, God-given talent that Whitney Houston was born with, she was, nonetheless, also a combination of influences. Religion, her culture, music, and, of course, her parents, were all part of the mix that made Whitney who she was. What her mother, Cissy, was able to offer was love, encouragement, and the schooling that comes from having been through it all herself.

Born in 1933, Cissy has had her own successful career in the music industry. At only five years old she was singing with her family in gospel bands, touring, and even appearing on TV. The Drinkard Four—or the Drinkard Singers, as they later became—were one of the most successful gospel acts of the era.

At age thirty, Cissy gave birth to Whitney, but was still able to work as a backup singer for acts such as Jimi Hendrix, Elvis Presley, the Drifters, Dusty Springfield, and many others. She also established her own solo career during the 1960s, constantly active on the music scene, which no doubt left an impression on her young daughter. Cissy had recorded five solo albums by 1980, by which point Whitney was seventeen and about to start her own meteoric rise.

When we meet Cissy in *I Wanna Dance with Somebody*, it is, fittingly, as she mentors her daughter about control—control over her voice and, really, her life. It is an important scene and one Denis O'Sullivan feels sets the tone for the entire film. "On *Bohemian Rhapsody*, Brian May said to me that if the audience doesn't forget five minutes in that they're not watching an actor as Freddie (Mecury) then the movie will never work. I think he said that in 2013. So, flash forward to 2018. We showed May, Roger (Taylor), and their wives the film for the first time and when it ended they all had tears in their eyes. And Brian, not remembering necessarily what he had said five years earlier, looked at me and said, 'Five minutes in I forgot I wasn't watching my friend.' When I watch this film, there's a particular scene where I go, 'Oh, this is our Whitney. This is it.' It's the third scene of the movie, where I just think the audience is gonna fall so in love with her. It's a scene where she's being drilled by her mom on

Opposite: Tamara Tunie as Cissy Houston, watching with pride as her daughter wows Clive Davis at Sweetwater's.

Below: Cissy and Bobby watching Whitney's monumental performance at the Billboard American Music Awards.

Overleaf: Cissy (Tamara) performing at Sweetwater's while Whitney (Naomi) sings backup. Director Kasi Lemmons: *"Cissy is a very important character to me. It's quite a beautiful character. She's both warm and hard."*

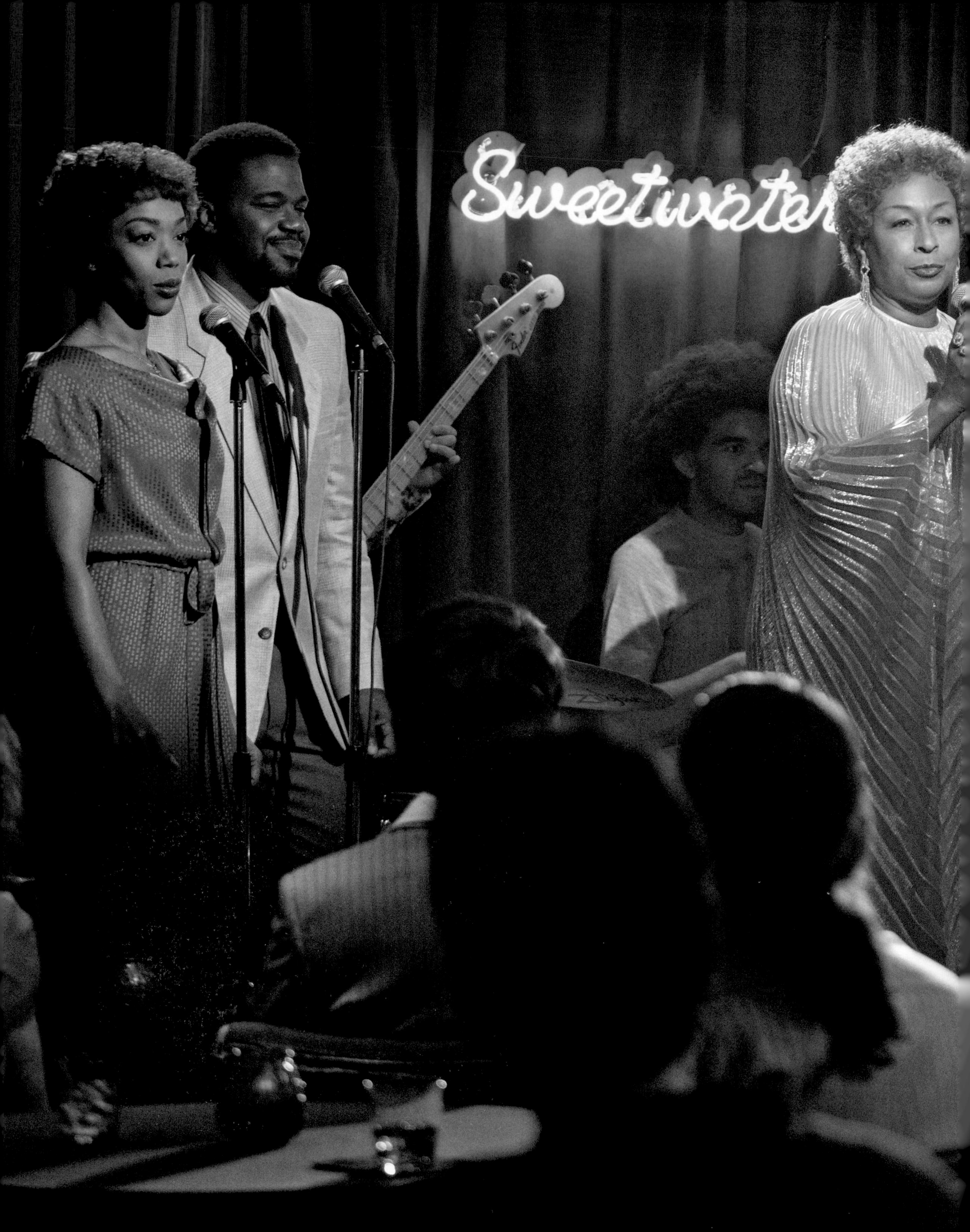
Sweetwate

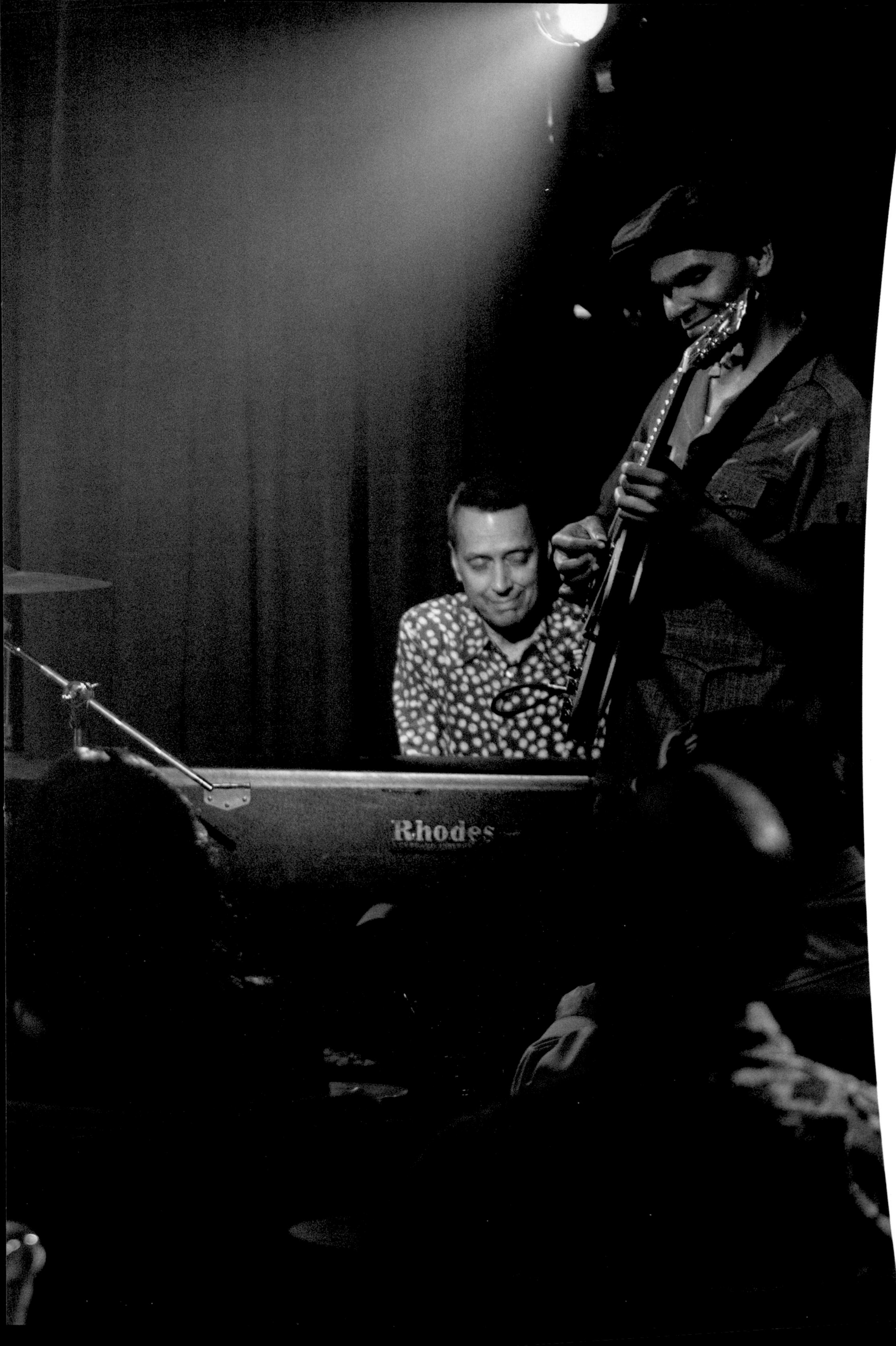
Rhodes

> "Whitney and Cissy were really fun scenes to do, it's a great relationship. One of the things I love about Anthony's writing—I was a fan of his before I came on this—is he has very actionable scenes."—Kasi Lemmons

singing gospel, and I think that performance by Tamara as her mom, and Naomi as Whitney, seals the deal. That's like, this is our Whitney and you're gonna love her and you're gonna be rooting for her and you're gonna want her to win."

Tamara Tunie commands the role of Cissy. A veteran of film and TV (perhaps best known for her role in *Law & Order: Special Victims Unit*), Tunie brings intelligence, passion, and steeliness to the part of Cissy. For the sound designers and engineers on the movie—who spent months sourcing music for reference—she was also able to offer something else: her voice.

"Robyn goes to Sweetwater's Club in New York and sees Whitney singing backing vocals for her mom," remembers supervising music and sound editor John Warhurst. "In that sequence, Cissy is singing. Tamara Tunie came to the studio and we recorded her version of that song. We were going to use Cissy's original version, but the problem was there was no multitrack of it. Rather than it being a stereo mix that you stick onto the film and see if you can get away with it, it's better when you have more control with the sound. So, we decided to give Tamara a try, and she really wanted a go. She's singing that song herself."

Cissy was a huge part of Whitney's life throughout her career and was constantly a force to be reckoned with. She is both loving and unashamedly uncompromising in that way only mothers can be. The film has to sell to the audience the belief that the people on the screen have known each other forever and know exactly how to support one another—and how to push one another's buttons. It helped when developing these interactions that Tunie and Lemmons had history, going back to Tunie's role as the narrator in Lemmons's directorial debut, *Eve's Bayou*, in 1997.

"Whitney and Cissy were really fun scenes to do," says Lemmons. "It's a great relationship. One of the things I love about Anthony's writing— I was a fan of his before I came on this—is he has very actionable scenes. They're these juicy scenes that actors want to do and are going to be able to really sink their teeth into; that's great to direct as well. It's just pure drama: He gets three people in a room and they're fighting and it's fantastic. I was definitely looking forward to those scenes."

The movie shows how much work Cissy put into helping her daughter develop her talent and become a star. These were scenes that both Naomi Ackie and Tamara Tunie loved—and looked forward to—doing.

JOHN HOUSTON
PORTRAYED BY CLARKE PETERS

Throughout Whitney's life, her father, John, was a powerful presence. Born in New Jersey in 1920, Houston worked at various occupations, including the army and politics, before finding the role that would define him—as the father and manager of Whitney. Houston actually established himself as an entertainment manager before Whitney rose to stardom, handling aspects of his wife's music career. Cissy and John's marriage would be rocked by infidelities, and they would eventually divorce, but not until after thirty-one years together. In his time as Whitney's manager, John would be there for her highest moments, but, arguably, did not offer the support he could have done for her lowest lows. Most famously, John Houston Entertainment LLC sued Whitney in 2002 for one hundred million dollars, citing money owed for various services the company had allegedly provided for her, including negotiating her hundred-million-dollar contract with Arista. Houston was famously quoted in December 2002 in *Celebrity Justice* stating, "You get your act together, honey, and you pay me the money that you owe me. If you do that, you haven't got a lawsuit."

One of the most complex characters in the movie—and in Whitney's life—is portrayed by veteran actor Clarke Peters. *Below*, he discusses a scene with director Kasi Lemmons. Lemmons: *"It'll be a familiar character to a lot of people, just because anyone that's had a kind of 'Tiger Mom and Dad' can kind of relate to it. But they loved her."*

In *I Wanna Dance with Somebody*, Houston is played by Clarke Peters, a stalwart actor of various films and TV shows, but perhaps best known for the television show *The Wire* and *Da 5 Bloods* (2020). The role of John Houston in the screenplay is a complex one, filled with moments of genuine affection, but also painful admissions, so the filmmakers needed an actor of Peters' caliber.

"There's no question that Cissy and John loved Whitney," says Kasi Lemmons. "Even John and what he did. I know he loved her. I believe that to be true. And yet, everybody's money was tied

"I think this was a loving, very loving family, very loving. But they were very hard on her and the situation was very hard." —Kasi Lemmons

up in Whitney Houston. She was the engine and the bank and the child and the princess; it's difficult to imagine what that does to a family."

The film does not shy away from the more poisonous aspects of the family dynamics. Indeed, they are crucial to the story of Whitney Houston, and it was also crucial to Kasi Lemmons, who was in a unique position, having had the chance to spend time with John and Whitney.

"I think this was a loving, very loving family, very loving," emphasizes Lemmons. "But they were very hard on her and the situation was very hard. We've seen this over and over again with many, many, many lovely stars and talents whose families are deeply involved in their business and their lives, and I couldn't imagine anything more hurtful, because I know that they loved each other. So, one of the reasons I was asking myself 'Am I going to take this job?' was that I knew Whitney. The first time I met Whitney, I met her father as well. And, so, I had a sense of them that was very clear, very much etched into memory. Let's say it was an interesting experience. They were exceptionally dynamic people. He was very concerned with their public persona, and then perhaps less concerned with what might have been going on privately. And, so, I was moved by meeting them. I wrote two scripts for her, one that I wrote with her in mind and then tried to get her to do it, and then another that I wrote for her for her company. So, I've certainly thought about her a lot, because I've written characters specifically for her to play and I had my own perspective on her and on John Houston. If the complexity of their relationship hadn't been in the *I Wanna Dance with Somebody* script, I would have wanted it in there, but it was there, and I was quite happy to see that."

Instability disturbing the stable home life Whitney so craves: John and Cissy argue, whilst hit records surround them on the walls (*below*). And as Whitney's career goes from strength to strength, John begins a new relationship outside of his marriage to Cissy (*opposite, bottom*).

Opposite, top: John's powerful presence is felt by Bobby Brown, as John lays down the law.

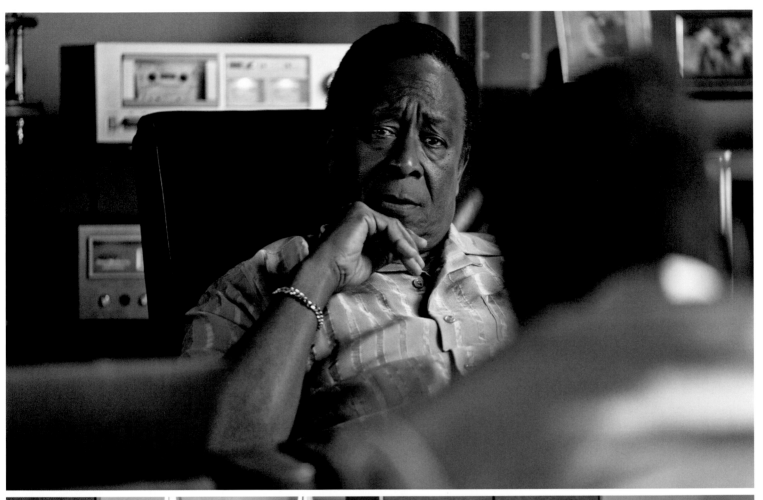

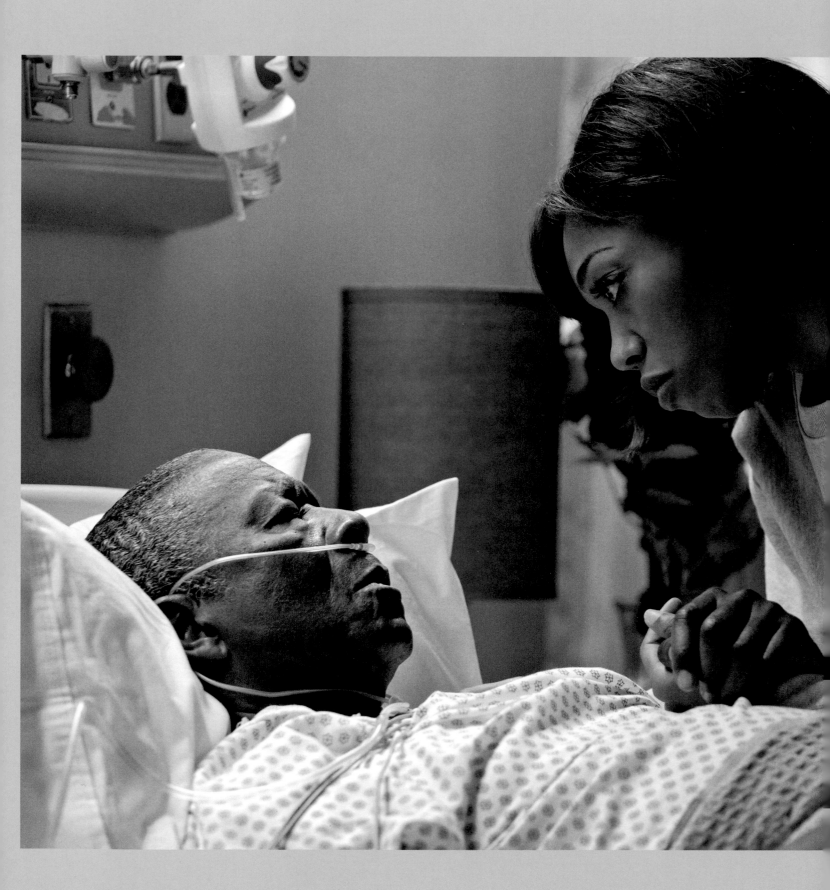

Conflict and support were equal parts of the Houston family dynamic. *Above,* Cissy and John giving their daughter support before her first nationally televised performance. *Left,* Whitney visiting her sickly father in the hospital turns into a bitter confrontation about the mismanagement of her money.

BOBBI KRISTINA
PORTRAYED BY BAILEE LOPES (BOBBI AGES 8-10)
AND BRIA DANIELLE SINGLETON

Denis O'Sullivan: "Whitney, three or four days before she passed, said to Pat, 'the only person in my life who has never let me down is Bobbi Kristina.'"

Bobbi Kristina Brown, the only child of Whitney Houston and Bobby Brown, was born March 4, 1993, the year after her parents married. Much like Whitney's own early exposure to the music industry via Cissy's career, Bobbi Kristina grew up in the showbiz world. Her mother would bring her on tour, with Bobbi Kristina even joining her on stage over the years. In the film, we see Whitney comforting Bobbi after a clash with her father; she treasures her daughter. Whether the family unit Whitney craves her whole life is a natural yearning or a societal expectation is irrelevant once Bobbi is born—Whitney truly loves Bobbi. The movie shows this legacy of love through a recurring motif: At three separate moments in the film we see what is described as a "mother-daughter tableau." First, with Cissy comforting a young Whitney in her lap, then Whitney singing gospel to Bobbi in her own lap, and then, finally, an older Bobbi soothing her own mother—simple intimacy and music saying more than a thousand oaths and platitudes.

"From the moment Bobbi was born, she was the center of Whitney's life," explains Anthony McCarten. "I tried to reflect that in this film and show how, toward the end of Whitney's life, the home they built together was the closest Whitney came to her dream homelife."

The legacy of love: Throughout the film, the recurring theme of the mother-daughter tableau shifts from Whitney being Bobbi Kristina's rock, to Bobbi being Whitney's source of comfort. Pat Houston: *"I love the private moments that she had with Bobbi Kristina. It's very hard when you're so close to the subject and you know her life better than anyone on the set."*

> "Ultimately, one of the breakthroughs for Anthony and me, or at least for me, was when we hit on the idea that she finds home in her daughter, and her daughter becomes the person she wants to live for and to show who the best version of herself is." —Denis O'Sullivan

O'Sullivan emphasizes this further, explaining how crucial the idea of "home" was and how the lessons learned on their previous movie, *Bohemian Rhapsody*, informed *I Wanna Dance with Somebody*. "At scripting stage, we had to define what the movie was about. What's the core? I learned working on *Jersey Boys* and then *Bohemian* that you have to be able to remove the music and still have a compelling story. You can't have a soundtrack in search of a movie. You need a movie with a great soundtrack. That was the challenge of breaking it down to a fundamental, human level. With Whitney, it was this idea of a woman who has a preternatural talent, but who is seeking to find home and define home for herself. She keeps trying to do it: first with Robyn, and then 'home' becomes about buying a big house, because she can, and then she tries with Bobby. Ultimately, one of the breakthroughs for Anthony and me, or at least for me, was when we hit on the idea that she finds home in her daughter, and her daughter becomes the person she wants to live for and to show who the best version of herself is."

At the movie's climax, Bobbi is in the crowd for her mother's greatest achievement. She does not see "Whitney Houston" on stage; she sees her mom.

Bobbi Kristina Brown died from lobar pneumonia on July 26, 2015, at the age of twenty-two.

Opposite, top: Naomi Ackie hugging the young actress who portrays Bobbi Kristina as a child (Bailee Lopes); Bottom: Whitney and an older Bobbi Kristina (Bria Danielle Singleton) look at video clips of Whitney's legendary performances online and see the outpouring of adoration from fans across the world.

Above: Naomi holding baby Bobbi.

Right: Director Kasi Lemmons gives direction and support to Bailee Lopes during an emotionally difficult scene, as Kris Sidberry (portraying Pat Houston) looks on.

Overleaf: Bobbi Kristina (Bria Danielle Singleton) and Whitney share a private, happy moment.

CHAPTER 3
I'M EVERY WOMAN
THE HAIR AND MAKEUP

" So, for me, I felt like it was my job as a storyteller to tell the story through hair to make this interesting for the audience. I wanted to make sure that the story was well told, so I used a lot of reference photos to get me to the point where I wanted it to be. And from there, I did my best to bring those wigs to life. "

—Brian Badie

Previous page: Naomi as Whitney, the morning after the night with Eddie Murphy (portrayed by Jimmie Fails).

Above: Makeup Department Head Tisa Howard working on Naomi to create Whitney's look. The mirror is covered with images of Whitney for reference. Howard: *"I had all my research in chronological order to show the progression, the evolution of Whitney. I had all my pictures on boards for reference and I would put a board right on my counter and have it side-by-side with what makeup I'm doing."*

Right, top: Tisa Howard at the makeup table.

Right, bottom: Hair Department Head Brian Badie with Whitney's many wigs. Badie: *"Sometimes we did like four changes in a day. Whitney alone had twenty-eight wigs throughout the film. It was a lot of hair. That's the most I've ever done on one character, and I've been doing this since 1995."*

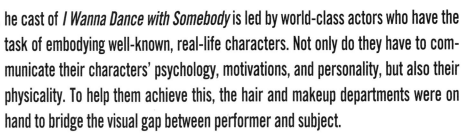

The cast of *I Wanna Dance with Somebody* is led by world-class actors who have the task of embodying well-known, real-life characters. Not only do they have to communicate their characters' psychology, motivations, and personality, but also their physicality. To help them achieve this, the hair and makeup departments were on hand to bridge the visual gap between performer and subject.

For Tisa Howard, the department head for makeup, the starting point was breaking down the script, creating timelines and image boards for each character. "I was at my dining-room table for a month and a half just breaking down that whole script, reading it inside and out, creating timelines—timelines for her age, timelines for the performances. When I read the script, I read at least forty looks, and that would include iconic looks, performances, and everyday styles. I had to simplify that so that I wouldn't go crazy. I had to make sure that I document everything and make a board that's going to cover all the iconic looks that we're covering in the movie. That means I have to go and do the research and get pictures and get the makeup and figure out, Okay, I have to stay true to these looks…. Whitney's most iconic looks in the movie are 'How Will I Know,' 'It's Not Right but It's Okay,' 'I Will Always Love You,' the Super Bowl, and the American Music Awards performance."

Brian Badie, the department head for hair, had a team of three people working on the looks for the entire cast. "I literally designed every character in the film," recalls Badie. "But then I oversee and delegate and my team have their own responsibilities. So I didn't physically do everyone's hair, but I basically had to make sure everything came together perfectly for the film. I was responsible for Whitney/Naomi. I did all her looks personally. Then I did Bobby Brown and Eddie Murphy and a lot of the male characters because I'm a barber as well…. Primarily my job was Whitney because she was in every scene in the movie, I think, except for one. All my days were occupied with her. We would average sometimes three to four looks a day."

If the audience looks at the movie screen and does not buy the actor's transformation into the character, then the suspension of disbelief is broken—they will no longer be empathizing with Whitney Houston; their mind will be elsewhere. Costuming, writing, dialect, acting—all this and more are needed to sell a convincing biopic. By getting the makeup as authentic as possible, not only will it, ideally, blend in seamlessly and be accepted unquestioningly by the viewer, but it will also give the actor the confidence that they have the exact tools they need to perform. In her search for verisimilitude, Tisa Howard left no stone unturned, as she explains:

"Whitney had one lipstick she was loyal to, and it was called Cranberry Kiss, and it was a lipstick that [her makeup artist] Roxanna always rolled her eyes at—'Oh, gosh, she's

Whitney had one lipstick she was loyal to, and it was called Cranberry Kiss, and it was a lipstick that [her makeup artist] Roxanna always rolled her eyes at—'Oh, gosh, she's gonna put this on again'—but she always felt dressed up with that lipstick and her sunglasses on." —Tisa Howard

Left: Getting Whitney's signature looks just right was paramount—even down to her Cranberry Kiss lipstick.

Above: Accuracy in the music videos was also important: Here the makeup department matched the dark cherry-brown nail polish to the original video for "It's Not Right but It's Okay." Tisa Howard: "*She was relatable to young people and she was relatable to older people. She stayed on trend when it comes to fashion and hair. Her hair changed a lot, but she was always on trend.*"

gonna put this on again'—but she always felt dressed up with that lipstick and her sunglasses on. It was by Fashion Fair, and it was a primary-reddish color lipstick and it had a little bit of a shimmer. Her nails as well; I checked each time do these performances have nails done? Because when you look at anything on the Internet, she wasn't really about her nails. I would have a nail board to show how her nails were to prove that she didn't have them done. But if we did have iconic looks with the nails done, which there were three looks in the movie, I made sure her nails were done exactly like what she did back at that time. Nails and lips. For example, in 'It's Not Right,' she had dark-colored nails, like they were in the video. It was a dark, brownish color, in the family of colors from Wicked by Essie, to be exact, or like a black cherry chutney. I put that on her fingernails and toenails. Her wedding was another thing that is in the movie that was documented online. If you google it, she has her nails done. And it was a champagne, warm color, copper tone. We put that on her nails. The other we did, I think, was the American Music Awards ceremony.... The Internet is your best friend. I had that in front of me the whole time."

Similar to Tisa Howard, Brian was able to find many references online, as Whitney was so publicized her entire career. But Brian used these photos more as a jumping-off point

Above: Whitney had dozens of looks in her life; in the movie, Hair Department Head Brian Badie tells her story through several different wigs and hairstyles.

for how he needed to bring everything together across the entire film's running time. He was able to add in his own initiative rather than mechanically re-creating each look and checking them off one after the other.

"It was about reference photos," confirms Brian, "and trying to decide which hair story to go with for the script, because Whitney changed her hair so much. If it wasn't an iconic moment, then it was about deciding which look would be best to tell the story for the film …if it's 1989, for example, Whitney could have possibly in her real life had fifteen hairstyles in that year. So, for me, I felt like it was my job as a storyteller to tell the story through hair to make this interesting for the audience. There are also hairstyles that maybe the audience might not be familiar with, so my thinking was maybe that's a good thing—to show some kind of range so we can introduce some looks that the audience might not be aware of. I feel like I wanted to make sure that the story was well told, so I used a lot of reference photos to get me to the point where I wanted it to be. And from there, I did my best to bring those wigs to life."

The movie is a period piece. While it is set in the recent past, changes in style, advancements in technology, and access to period-specific materials present the hair and makeup departments with advantages and disadvantages.

"I feel like you try to stay as true to the look as possible," confirms Badie. "The way I drew the line [on recreating a hairstyle exactly] is what we know today as hair stylists, as opposed to what they were doing in the '80s or the '90s. I feel like we're more revolutionary

Top: Styling another Whitney look. Brian Badie: *Naomi was a complete professional … I can't imagine the pressure she was under. When she sat in my chair, I tried to be whatever she needed me to be at the moment—to offer her any type of support emotionally that can help her get through the day."*

Bottom: The work didn't stop with Whitney: here, Badie works with Ashton Sanders to recreate Bobby Brown's signature asymmetrical wedge hairstyle.

The makeup and hair departments had their work cut out for them, creating several different looks for Robyn Crawford (Nafessa Williams, *above and opposite top*); Eddie Murphy (Jimmie Fails, with Naomi Ackie, *top*), and Cissy Houston (Tamara Tunie, *opposite bottom*). Brian Badie: *"What I found interesting was she had these really big curly looks—I call them poodle looks. Really big, curly, poofy hair that she used a lot in the mid-80s, around the time when she was dating Eddie Murphy. We found loads of paparazzi photos that I thought she looked really beautiful in. I don't feel like a lot of audiences know this hair look."*

in hairstyling and wig application than we were back twenty to thirty years ago. A lot of times Whitney probably used weaves or hair extensions, so that will be an instance when I can take total creative freedom and say, 'Okay, I can't use a weave so I will use a wig in this particular situation.' It's just more functional for filming as well, because the weave is more permanent; a wig I can take off throughout the day and switch them up … I feel like there are certain things I just didn't want to compromise as an artist, as well. So, if I felt like something from back then could have been maybe improved upon or changed a little bit, then I would. There are also other personal things that I find as an artist I would like to do for myself because I don't want to plagiarize."

Adapting the Looks

I Wanna Dance with Somebody is not about mimicry. It's not simply an exercise in matching the real-life people and events like for like; the film is telling a story and it is embodying the people and moments from Whitney Houston's life through this prism, rather than a static museum exhibition. As such, Tisa Howard and Brian Badie could not just put the exact makeup and hair on the actors that their real-life counterparts wore and send them onto set; they had to adapt every look to fit the specific actor.

"We know that Whitney and Naomi are not twins," says Howard. "They don't look alike. They are both beautiful in their own way. They both have beautiful features. But what I would do is capture Whitney through Naomi's eyes. Naomi has fuller lips than Whitney, so instead of going with the two colors that we would normally apply, like reds or dark colors, I would lighten up the color a little bit to adjust accordingly to Naomi's lips, so it won't be so distracting and still kind of stayed in the same category as Whitney's. As far as her nose, I shaded her nose a touch, just to give her that little bit of a point, but not too much.

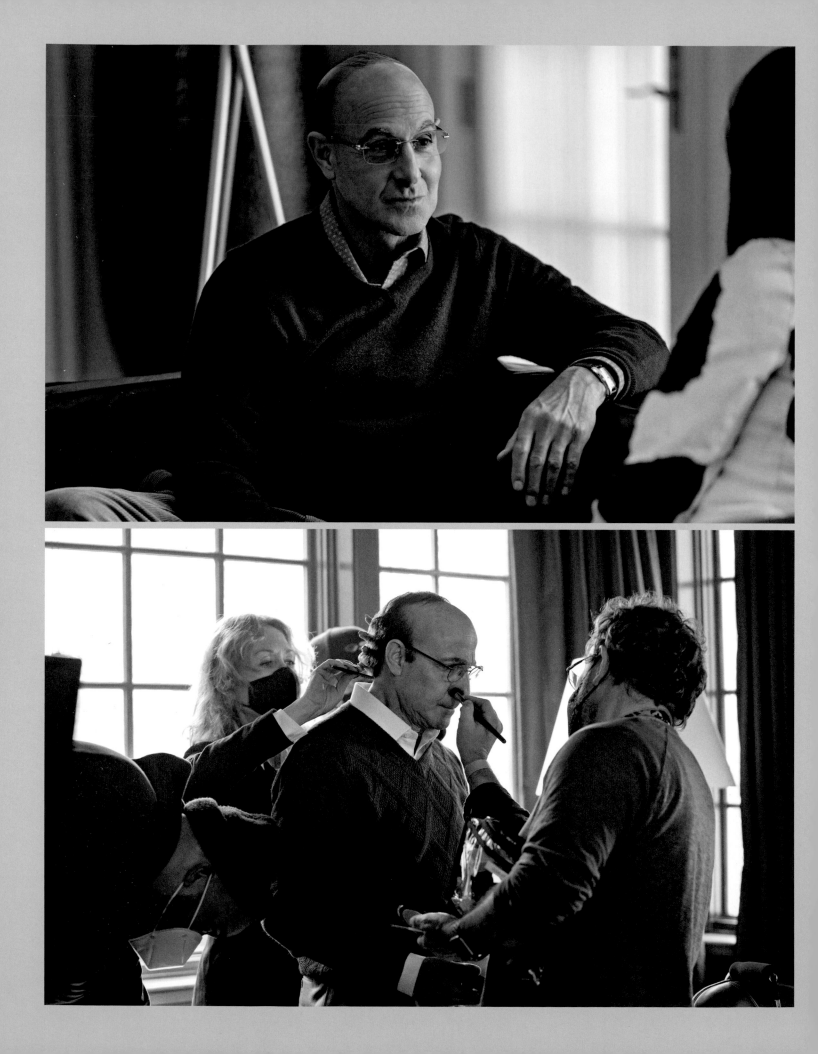

> "I had a special effects artist, Craig Lindberg, who made sure that the aging and everything was accurate; he's on top of that. We did a lot of the aging with painting and shading. We didn't really use prosthetics."
>
> —Tisa Howard

I captured Whitney through her eyes, creating more of a lid for Naomi, because she doesn't have the same eyes as Whitney, but they were easy to shade."

Badie had similar challenges: "That's a daily thing because neck length, facial structure, forehead size, everything comes into play when it comes to haircuts. A bang on Whitney could be longer or shorter than it would be on Naomi. That is the type of thing that I have to alter through cutting. I think also hair color: If we're going into the auburn family, Whitney's undertones and Naomi's undertones might be different. So, where Whitney might have a more yellow or golden undertone, Naomi would be more red. I needed to counter that in the coloring to make sure that it contrasts her complexion well. If I went too copper, and if her undertones didn't match, it could run the risk of making her look jaundiced, or making her look too ashy for camera, which will then affect the makeup and costuming as well. That's where as an artist you have to know how to incorporate and use certain techniques that work for Naomi physically, but that didn't really match on Whitney, but still stayed within the realm of re-creating a look."

The Aging Challenge

As the characters age across three decades, the viewer needs to see them mature and change and understand that time has passed. The challenge this presents is to do it in a way that is true to life, but also so the audience can still recognize the same character twenty or thirty years older.

"I had a special effects artist, Craig Lindberg, who made sure that the aging and everything was accurate; he's on top of that," explains Howard. "We did a lot of the aging with painting and shading. We didn't really use prosthetics.

"The great thing about Clive is that he's played by Stanley Tucci, who kind of has a little bit of the resemblance. So, it was awesome to paint on Stanley. Stanley is all about his acting, so he contributed to the role, too, and we didn't have to alter too much for him. If we did anything with

Opposite: Transforming Stanley Tucci into Clive Davis.

Below: Naomi (*center*), aged for the the camera. Tisa Howard: *"When it comes to the real Whitney, we were so busy looking from the outside and judging or just ignoring or whatever, and this person was actually just crying for help. And she was lonely, you know? We were taking, taking, taking to a certain extent for our entertainment but we didn't realize what she was going through personally as far as exhaustion and always aiming to please. But she was still strong, still marching to the beat of her own drum. She wasn't a pushover."*

Transforming Naomi from a Jersey girl (*right*) into a budding singer (*opposite*) and, finally into a superstar (*top*).

"What we did was with, say, the drug abuse or the exhaustion, we would create wrinkles around her eyes or do some type of wear and tear around the mouth—where it was documented that she had had that. I made sure I'd done my research."—Tisa Howard

Above: Tisa Howard giving Naomi a touchup.

Opposite: Recreating looks isn't always about glamour. An exhausted Whitney is created by flattening the wigs so they don't look as fresh, and using makeup for a tired-eye effect.

aging, it would be maybe a wrinkle here or coloring, a lot of painting. For Cissy, we would age Tamara, make her young and then older. Just by creating the wrinkles and going under the eyes you can see the age progression. But Whitney has the really big change compared with everyone else."

While Whitney's look did evolve as she grew older, there were not great fluctuations in weight or major reinventions. Whitney in her twenties is not dramatically different from Whitney in her thirties. Communicating the changes had to be subtle. With this in mind, the crew took a sensitive approach to showing Houston through her struggles with drugs.

"What we did was with, say, the drug abuse or the exhaustion," details Howard, "we would create wrinkles around her eyes or do some type of wear and tear around the mouth—where it was documented that she had had that. I made sure I'd done my research."

Similarly, Brian Badie decided to not overplay any kind of deterioration with the look of Whitney in her later years. Any noticeable change in her hair, for instance, was minimal because, as Badie explains, "she always wore wigs and we've learned from that. What I did was build it up to build it down. So, I styled the hair as it was, but then I might add some water for times when she was sweating a lot. I added oil-based product to make the wig look flatter and not as fresh. We didn't go as downtrodden as people might have seen Whitney in some of her footage. I personally didn't want to go that hard core because I wanted to stay respectful about this. I felt like everybody was on the same page. So, I don't feel like we made her look really bad. I feel like we told the story to give the audience an idea that she was struggling with drug abuse, but I don't feel like we needed to go the messy route like, say, reality TV. I think we kept it

Above: The look created for the "Run to You" video.

nice and respectful for her because we want it to be a good legacy. It wasn't trash. This isn't a trash film. This is a film to celebrate Whitney."

Whitney means something to every person working on the film. But for Tisa Howard, there was a personal connection—and a responsibility that came with it.

"My mentor, Roxanna Floyd, used to do Whitney. Roxanna and Kevyn Aucoin were Whitney's two favorite makeup artists. But Roxanna was definitely a confidant and close friend of Whitney and also a makeup artist and she lost her life during the last tour. That tour was dedicated to Roxanna. She was in the back of the program of the tour. But when Roxanna started to get sick she passed the torch to Janina Lee and then Janina starts to take care of Whitney until Whitney passed away. So, I would ask her specific details, like 'What kind of makeup did you use for this' or 'What was her favorite lipstick?' I couldn't have done this movie without Janina. It was meant to be, and it was perfect for both of us, because it was like the 'six degrees of separation.' And it was like we were aiming to please two people who were connected, and that was Roxanna and that was Whitney. The journey was very special for both of us."

TISA HOWARD ON THE SUPER BOWL

"The look that I was most intimidated by was the Super Bowl. That look is so simple, but the pressure on me was that this was going to be the opening of the movie. This is the time where you have to get that audience and lock them in. So, it was important to come as close as possible to the Whitney look, because when the viewer sees Naomi, they have to see Whitney from the start, and then hold on to them. Once you get them in the beginning, you've got them for the rest of the movie. You're gonna get them because of the actor, you're gonna get them because of the performances, the look, the cinematography, everything is going to pull people in. But that initial moment of her coming on screen is when you capture the audience, and that was the pressure—and I was scared. But the look that I was most afraid of was the look that I did really well—that's what Janina said! She said, 'You were so afraid of it, then, man, you knocked it out of the park!' I'm still on the edge. I don't know if I did it right."

CHAPTER 4

RUN TO YOU
THE COSTUMES

" I realized how simple her taste was, how much of a Jersey girl she was, and how much of a streetwear queen she was in terms of all the cool outfits and accessories. She had every Nike sneaker, every Air Jordan, you know; sweatsuits, tracksuits, visors. How she put her looks together when she wasn't working was so iconic and influenced a lot of what women were wearing, casually, particularly Black woman, during that time. That's how we dressed. "

—Charlese Antoinette Jones

"**P**eople idolize Whitney," says costume designer Charlese Antoinette Jones. "They love Whitney and they are so protective of her image. I just wanted to make sure when we were re-creating these music videos, when we were re-creating the stage performances, everything was exact. The details were right."

Charlese Antoinette Jones joined the production just before shooting started. Some of the groundwork had already been done, but Jones had just two days to redesign the whole movie. And, unfortunately, there were not a lot of personal artifacts to work from.

"Whitney had storage units that flooded," explains Jones, "and then also storage units that she lost due to financial issues. So, we didn't really have pieces in her own personal archive to pull from. We were able to source some pieces that vintage dealers told us were hers at one point, or were of that period. I sourced lots of Dolce & Gabbana from the early 2000s that felt like things she was wearing during that time. They weren't the exact clothes, but they were in the same runway collection. We have really good relationships with vintage dealers and vendors, and we'd send them pictures of her during particular eras and they would find things and send them to us.... We ended up re-creating a lot of stuff and sourcing things vintage."

Whitney Houston is often referred to as "the Voice," and her once-in-a-generation vocal ability is likely the first thing many think of when they think of her; but hand in hand with her singing is her styling. Whitney was a formidable presence on the stage and in videos, and her fashion was perfectly calibrated to complement and enhance her performances. The first major hits of her career were in the 1980s, and much of the costume department's work focused on that period.

Jones remembers: "There was a decent stock of '80s clothing that had been amassed. So, I just went through and took everything apart and went on a scavenger hunt to find things that felt like her during that period. I really wanted to be able to distinguish between her growing up and being really young and youthful in the beginning of the

Below: The bow that started it all: adding the now-iconic touch to Naomi's costume for the "How Will I Know" music video.

Opposite: The sophisticated look of a star.

"I was blessed to have a lot of great resources for '80s clothing to be able to do that. To be able to pull up these amazing dresses and pieces and all these fun metallics and build some more dresses."—Charlese Antoinette Jones

early '80s to her getting some money and what that looks like in her clothing. Her clothing would change and become bigger: For instance, sleeves are bigger, she's wearing more metallics. There's a whole montage that shows her getting different plaques and bottles of Dom Pérignon, things like that, and I wanted to show through clothing the time jumps and money jumps even, you know, based on how she's dressed in this montage. I was blessed to have a lot of great resources for '80s clothing to be able to do that. To be able to pull up these amazing dresses and pieces and all these fun metallics and build some more dresses. We built some really beautiful pieces for scenes with her and Bobby Brown. Some beautiful leather jackets and sequined gowns and things like that show they are rock stars. I really wanted to show that she was an iconic pop star and I wanted her look to reflect that, particularly at the height of her career."

Like all great pop stars, Whitney had key, showstopping looks that have become iconic, and the costume department faced a challenge. Not only did they have to make the outfits from scratch at times, and make them accurate, but the clothes also had to fit Naomi and fit within the overall aesthetic of the movie. One highly publicized piece that will feature in the movie is the "matador jacket" by South African designer Marc Bouwer.

Clothing with a metallic flair was used to show Whitney's ascent; as her fame increases and she comes into more money, her clothes become more upscale and elaborate. Charlese Antoinette Jones: *"It was the early to mid-80s when she started blowing up so we needed the shoulders. In some instances we needed the metallics and we needed those like primary colors to pop. We needed these weird synthetic fabrics. Like we've never used in that way before. It was all used to signify where we were placed in time. But I think it's all about how it was done, and I think I did a good job of balancing it and having fun with it."*

"We re-created the black and gold matador jacket. "I ended up meeting Marc Bouwer, who actually designed a lot of those matador jackets and most of her stage and tour looks. I was showing him photos and he was so excited."—Charlese Antoinette Jones

Left: The sketch for the famous matador jacket.

Opposite, top: The jacket being built in the costumer's studio.

Opposite, bottom: The jacket as it appeared in the film.

The Matador Jacket

"We re-created the black and gold matador jacket," Jones confirms. "I ended up meeting Marc Bouwer, who actually designed a lot of those matador jackets and most of her stage and tour looks. I was showing him photos and he was so excited.

"I did tweak some things. The shape of the jacket is a little different. On Naomi it's longer than the one Whitney wore, and it's not a true matador style. The fit is a little different. It's shaped differently because I found when I was putting true '80s style pieces on Naomi, there was some resistance because everybody has this slightly negative feeling toward the shoulder pads of the '80s. So, we didn't put crazy shoulder pads in that jacket. I was able to sneak some in here and there on other pieces, but I had to scale the size back. For instance, instead of it being perhaps one and a half inches, maybe this shoulder pad was three-quarters of an inch."

"I love to be able to watch something and then someone show me the real image and to be, 'Oh, wow, they did such a good job re-creating that.' That's the kind of feeling I wanted to give to people watching this film."

—Charlese Antoinette Jones

Every detail of the outfit from the "It's Not Right but It's Okay" music video was replicated, from the choker and black leather glove (*above*) to the chain accents on the dress and wide-strap sandal, which was created from scratch by a cobbler. Tisa Howard: *"For 'It's Not Right' I wanted to really do it justice … I really wanted to do it right so I even played on my own face to make sure. I hit it on the nail and I was really proud of it. I was smiling the whole day watching and tracking and making sure that it would stay perfect the whole day. But I was really, really proud that I really stretched myself."*

Throughout Whitney's career, fans around the world would pore over every music video, every magazine spread, and scrutinize every aspect of Whitney's appearance. With the amount of reference images available at the click of a button nowadays, it is easy for anyone to see exactly what Whitney was wearing. These are the sorts of details that matter to fans and that Jones was determined to get right.

Charlese Antoinette Jones remembers, "I came in and made sure things matched. For 'It's Not Right but It's Okay' we made that choker match exactly. We made the glove match exactly. We even made her shoes, because those shoes don't exist anymore. We found a shoe, took off the strap, added another strap; there was a thin strap in the front and a wide strap toward the instep. We had a cobbler remake the shoe. Literally, a lot of what I did was going through every single look we were re-creating with a fine-tooth comb, zooming in, really honing in and really wanting things to match. We definitely took some creative liberties in terms of fabrics. I love to be able to watch something and then someone show me the real image and to be, 'Oh, wow, they did such a good job re-creating that.' That's the kind of feeling I wanted to give to people watching this film."

"How she put her looks together when she wasn't working was so iconic and influenced a lot of what women were wearing, casually, particularly Black women, during that time. That's how we dressed." —Charlese Antoinette Jones

Whitney's clothes tell the story of her life. The film is about Whitney the person, not just Whitney the singer, and much of the running time is spent with her just being herself, not dressing for anyone else. Setting the tone of her everyday look was crucial to Jones. "I realized how simple her taste was, how much of a Jersey girl she was, and how much of a streetwear queen she was in terms of all the cool outfits and accessories. She had every Nike sneaker, every Air Jordan, you know; sweatsuits, tracksuits, visors. How she put her looks together when she wasn't working was so iconic and influenced a lot of what women were wearing, casually, particularly Black woman, during that time. That's how we dressed."

Dressing the Rest

The main focus was, of course, Whitney, but beyond her, Charlese and her team also had to design, make costumes, or source outfits for all the supporting cast as well as background players. "There could be 500 people in a scene—we fit them all. Some of them in advance, some of them on the day. For the South Africa concert, in particular, it had to be specific; that performance looks different from other performances. We had a whole separate background team that was constantly doing fittings and sending me photos. I would give them notes and they would have to either rework outfits or, if there were big background days, I would go in on the day of shooting and help and give direction and show them what I wanted to make the process go faster. We fitted every single person in every scene."

Costumes evoke a feeling and a time—from the flash of Whitney and Bobby's engagement party (*left, top*), to hanging out in New Jersey and even at her father's office, every character's costumes evoke the diversity of mid-1980s fashion.

> " I had a great team of assistants. I designed a bunch of Bobby Brown's looks from scratch, either in-house or outsourced. Leather and custom-made denim. Lots of leather jackets. Lots of suits as well."—Charlese Antoinette Jones

Dressing Bobby Brown

"I had a great team of assistants," remembers costume designer Charlese Antoinette Jones. "I designed a bunch of Bobby Brown's looks from scratch, either in-house or outsourced. Leather and custom-made denim. Lots of leather jackets. Lots of suits as well. We made this really cool silver suit that he wears in the '80s with an amazing trapezoid shape. You know how those jackets were back then—so good. We were able to do big shoulders on him. For some reason on him, it wasn't as severe as it was on Naomi. That was a lot of fun. A lot of fun. I designed all the characters in the film. I really don't know how I did it. I'm still tired."

From casual leather jackets and baseball caps to tailored suits, Bobby's outfits were designed by costume designer Charlese Antoinette Jones and custom made.

Below: Costume sketches for Bobby's black leather suit for the Soul Train Awards scene *(left)*, and tailored white suite for the scene in which he meets with John Houston in his office *(right)*.

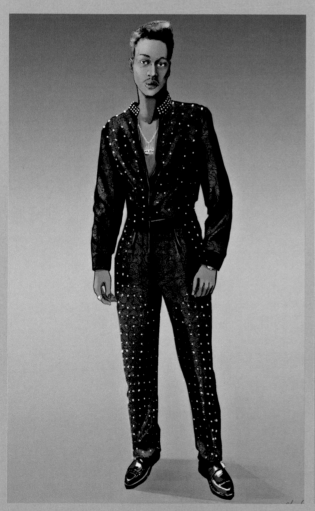

CHARLESE ANTOINETTE JONES ON DRESSING THE SOUL TRAIN AWARDS

"We made a lot of things for Robyn. We made this beautiful fuchsia-pink, metallic suit for her for the Soul Train Awards that I'm super proud of… I changed everything everyone was wearing from real life at those awards because I felt like I wanted the look to be a little bit more 'up.' We found this amazing beaded dress from a dealer in New York and I put Naomi in it. I mean, it's just insane. I thought, 'She has to wear this dress for the Soul Train Awards because what Whitney was actually wearing was a bit more casual,' and during the '80s, style was more casual than it is now. It was the first or second year of the Soul Train Awards, so it was very early in its inception. But I was like, I don't care. I wanted to be glamorous—let's go all out and have fun. You know? That was the only part of the movie where I took a lot of liberties, but it was because I wanted to punch it up a notch. So, everybody looks really dope.

Even Cissy's dress—I ended up using a Halston gown for it and adding a bunch of stuff to the gown to make it feel more early '80s. I added this amazing embellishment to the shoulder, and the actress, Tamara, who plays Cissy, one day she texts me footage of the real Cissy literally wearing the same dress with the accent on it. And she said, 'Did you know this?' And I said, 'No.' Literally, the same fuchsia-pink with rhinestones coming down the shoulder. I didn't know Cissy had worn it, but I knew that dress because my mom had a dress like that. My grandma had a dress like that. Theirs were blue, but that one-shoulder Grecian dress was a thing. And it just so happened that I used the exact color Cissy wore. There were lots of amazing, happy coincidences like that. I find as a designer my intuition is so important to rely on; in this instance, in particular, I had to, because I didn't have time not to. I just told myself: You know this period. Just do what you know. What would a woman that age be wearing? She would have a Halston gown from the late '70s.

We re-created Bobby Brown's look, and for his dancers, we built everything from head to toe. He had on this amazing white trench coat and we re-created that. He and his dancers wore these pale-gray, matching button-downs and slacks. I'm really proud of that scene in particular, because everyone looks just amazing."

Clockwise, from top left: Naomi's vintage beaded gown and Nafessa in the custom-made pink lame suit; a closeup of the extraordinary beading on the vintage dress; Tamara in vintage Halston; Ashton's custom-made re-creation of Bobby's iconic white trench coat and gray suit.

"I definitely feel like her choices were very, very intentional. There's a lot of respectability and politics at play. Particularly during that time, she was dealing with being sold as this cookie-cutter pop star, which her community was not loving, so there was that fight. I feel like that really reflects on how she presented on stage. She was a different person."—Charlese Antoinette Jones

Whitney's On-Stage Style

Beyond the actual costumes themselves and how they worked on camera or on stage, Whitney's style throughout her career said a lot about who she was as a major Black female performer in the eighties and nineties. As Jones discusses, "I definitely feel like her choices were very, very intentional. There's a lot of respectability and politics at play. Particularly during that time, she was dealing with being sold as this cookie-cutter pop star, which her community was not loving, so there was that fight. I feel like that really reflects on how she presented on stage. She was a different person. You know, they said on stage she's 'Whitney Houston'; off stage, she was Nippy. You can just see that. We've watched some documentaries and you see how she's putting on a persona—an act. She wasn't super/overtly sexy. She came out of the church. It's not like she was Madonna, during that time. So, that's also really reflected in how she dressed. She's very covered. She wore gowns. She was very elegant. It was definitely like a particular way of thinking about how to present as a Black woman during that time, and I think we all do it."

Whitney's regal, elegant onstage style elevated her stage persona, making her stand out among other female performers of the time, and raising her to icon status.

Overleaf: Whitney's incredible wedding gown created by fashion designer Marc Bouwer was reported to have cost $40,000. Photos of it were studied in order to faithfully re-create it for the film.

CHAPTER 5

WHERE DO BROKEN HEARTS GO
THE SETS

" By re-creating these locations and the atmosphere of the world, it really pays off. And it's helpful for the actors as well, having the reality of what they need right there. For Stanley to spend time in the office and feel like it's his domain—he just ate it up. "

—Matt Jackson

I Wanna Dance with Somebody is the largest independent film ever to shoot in Massachusetts. Except for two days spent in Los Angeles, the entire movie was shot in and around Boston. It was a fifty-day schedule from September to December 2021, mostly based on a soundstage at Marina Studios.

Previous page: The set for the "How Will I Know?" music video.

Below: The interior of the Houston home.

Opposite, top: Whitney, Clive, John, and Cissy meet in Clive Davis's office.

Opposite, bottom: Re-creating the set of a television interview.

"We basically did all our construction for the film there," recalls producer Matt Jackson. "We built Clive's bungalow at the Beverly Hills Hotel, we built his office, we built the recording studios, the interior of the Beverly Hills, then we built Whitney's suite in the Beverly Hills where she passed away. So that was our home base, and we also had our production office there."

The soundstage catered to almost all their needs, even enabling them to re-create a desert scene where US military personnel watch Whitney sing the national anthem on television. It is standard procedure for a movie to film all the scenes they need on a set and then take it apart to build a new set. For *I Wanna Dance with Somebody*, the process was slightly more complicated, as some of the sets were needed throughout the film but also had to age and change over the three decades covered in the story.

"We used the spaces we could accordingly, and we're very mindful of that [change]," says Jackson. "A lot of the sets stayed in place, and they were there for most of the shoot, such as Clive's Beverly Hills bungalow. Clive's office was a set that we used constantly because it covers lots of different moments in the movie: It's where he signs her, it's where they're going over music, where they talk about her doing *The Bodyguard*—all that stuff was crucial for us.

Then, obviously, the recording studio stayed throughout the film because we kept dressing that differently for different times and periods. Those were our key sets."

So many of the sets were based on real places, and Jackson confirms it was "an obsession" to re-create them accurately. "I think you can sometimes become a slave to accuracy, but you need to make sure that the sets tie into the historical record, and production designer Gerald Sullivan did an excellent job. By re-creating these locations and the atmosphere of the world, it really pays off. And it's helpful for the actors as well, having the reality of what they need right there. For Stanley to spend time in the office and feel like it's his domain—he just ate it up."

What producer Josh Crook points out is the challenge of communicating a time period accurately, as opposed to bathing it in nostalgia or coloring it with lazy references that act as shorthand for certain decades. "For me, being true to the time was the biggest challenge. You have an idea what the '90s or the 2000s or the '80s

"For me, being true to the time was the biggest challenge. You have an idea what the '90s or the 2000s or the '80s and '70s were, but you have to be considerate of what the times were actually like, not just our memory of what we think the time period was. As we move through time, some of that archival stuff's forgotten or destroyed or lost."—Josh Crook

Above: The recording studio for a young Whitney. John Warhurst: *"We always joked with Naomi in the beginning: Whitney really is going to help you out. She's got your back."*

Right: The "Spider-web" stage used for the concert montage.

and '70s were, but you have to be considerate of what the times were actually like, not just our memory of what we think the time period was. As we move through time, some of that archival stuff's forgotten or destroyed or lost. Finding not just the set design references—the cars, that sort of thing—but also actual archival footage of Whitney—some companies whose material wasn't digital or hadn't been digitized just had warehouses full of stuff. Those companies went under, or they were tired of paying the storage bills and they destroyed some amazing footage. We're very lucky that the estate has so much, but other places that were in charge of their own footage, it doesn't exist, you can't find it."

The movie contains several major set pieces, with Whitney performing in front of hundreds and even thousands of people. To do justice to these huge concerts, the production brought in some groundbreaking visual effects technology—a key piece of equipment dubbed "the black box."

"We shot the Super Bowl here in Boston in the winter, about as far away as you can get from Tampa in February," explains Crook. "The black box is an incredible piece of technology, which we immediately focused on. What our VFX producers and supervisors—the incredible Tim Field and Paul Norris—had done on *Bohemian Rhapsody* was an older process. It was using about eight cameras, and you shot 180 degrees of an actor. What we did was we shot individual actors in a ninety-camera setup. It's a 360-degree setup. The black box is actually a green box, and it's walled off with a green screen. Each actor sits down, claps, stands up, points, and you shoot them all around. We'll put thousands of them together and we can change their hair and their clothes so that each one looks like a different person. They become our Super Bowl audience. It's really incredible because that allows us to create 50,000 people at the Super Bowl in 1991. We shot it all at Gillette Stadium on a freezing-cold night. And we probably had, I think, 500 people there versus the 50,000 we needed. We closed them off and we replicated a bunch of the actions and did everything we needed to, but it will be a fully digital re-creation. We'll wipe out Gillette entirely, rebuild Tampa as a video effects piece with our audience. So, it's an absolutely incredible piece of technology, and I think we're either the first or second film to use it. It's kind of a burgeoning thing.

"Then in the middle of the field is Naomi, our actor, performing the national anthem with the color guard and security and everyone around her. So, we're shooting those simultaneously with green screen so we could wipe out the stadium behind her and in front of her.... Because I was budget conscious, an early idea was shooting in a field with spray-painted

lines standing in for the stadium, as it would have been a lot cheaper than renting out Gillette during football season. But, what makes Kasi so great at what she does, is she wanted us in a stadium so Naomi could feel what it would be like to have tens of thousands of people watching this small performance on this huge field and to get that perspective of the depth of it all. I do think it was absolutely the right call."

They were originally planning to use the black box on the Marina stage itself, but there wasn't enough depth, as they wanted to keep the other sets that were also there in the space at the same time. This included, as Jeff Kalligheri details, the set for the "How Will I Know" video, with all the incredible, colorful panels Whitney walks through, as well as the "Run to You" video from *The Bodyguard* sequence. "We also shot the entire 'It's Not Right but It's Okay' music video there. It's an exact replica. It looks amazing," affirms Kalligheri.

The money for this movie is there on the screen. *I Wanna Dance with Somebody* is the first movie to be released from Kalligheri and Denis O'Sullivan's Compelling Pictures production company, and it is a statement not just for them but for Whitney as well. While any film needs to be budget conscious, what Compelling Pictures has accounted for on this film is calibrated exactly for Whitney. "An agent asked me, 'How much are you making this for? Twenty-five million?'" recalls O'Sullivan. "I told him, no, it's more along the lines of

Right: Filming a concert scene; with the help of special effects, that small group of people will turn into a sell-out crowd.

Opposite, top: Filming the Soul Train Awards sequence.

Opposite, bottom: Filming outside in the freezing cold.

Bohemian Rhapsody's budget, which was above sixty. And he said, 'Really? Why? Whitney Houston didn't have big concerts, did she?' So, I looked at him and said, 'The Super Bowl?!' The South Africa concert was 170,000 people alone. I remember sitting with Anthony when he was working on the first draft of the script and I pitched the idea of having one of the first things we see be an open blue sky, and then three F-16s come into the frame. The reason was because I thought we should announce to the audience right off the bat that this is a big movie. This isn't a small biopic; this is an epic story for an icon."

Accordingly, it was a major shoot, incredibly labor intensive, especially for Naomi, who carries the film, and Kasi Lemmons, who was juggling other projects at the same time. For matching those Whitney performances, the crew would have Naomi performing, with the original Whitney footage side by side. "I'd kind of peek over and see if it was the actual video or Whitney's performance," Kasi remembers. "Naomi can't see can't see the monitor, but her performance is exact—hand movements, looks, everything. Naomi worked so hard to make sure she knew all of that every day. It was really incredible to see someone so dedicated, so exacting, and with the help of our choreographer and movement coach, James Alsop and Polly Bennett, respectively, she nailed it. It's kind of eerie, makes your hair stand up, especially because she's doing it for twelve hours a day, hitting it every time, which is not easy."

Kasi Lemmons had five weeks to prepare the film. Most lower-budget movies have more time to prep than that, never mind a film of this scale and budget. But Kasi had a level of passion, organization, and experience that elevated the film. Everything was so minutely prepared that when asked if anything had to radically change during the shoot, as is often the case, the only example Lemmons could recall was one of the few scenes they shot outside the soundstage, on location in Massachusetts. Even in this instance, which was the moment Bobby proposes to Whitney, it was the weather that changed its mind and nothing the filmmakers could have planned for. Kasi remembers: "[This movie] was a lot of interiors. We did shoot on a bridge when it was incredibly cold; twenty-seven degrees on a windy bridge. It wasn't planned, but we left the steam coming from the actors' mouths; it's still there because there was nothing saying that it had to be a warmer time. It kind of adds to the energy—but they were freezing."

CHAPTER 6

HOW WILL
I KNOW

THE VIDEOS
AND PERFORMANCES

" When I got the shooting schedule, I was like: I already know these videos, I already know these performances, when do we start dancing?! "

—James Alsop

Previous page: Naomi re-creating the dream sequence in the "Run to You" music video.

Opposite: Prelude to a star: we first see Whitney performing with the church choir (with her mother conducting), and then as backup singer for her mother at Sweetwater. Polly Bennett: *"I couldn't find anything of her being coached. I think her biggest coach was her mom watching her and how she performed. That's another thing we looked at: Cissy herself singing. We looked at Dionne Warwick singing. We looked to people that Whitney would have listened to when she was growing up to see the interplay that they have with the audience that she's then picked up."*

Below: Cinematographer Barry Ackroyd setting up the church scene.

Overleaf: Naomi performing in the concert montage, all exuberance and joy.

Whitney's was a career filled with an abundance of classic, era-defining songs and performances, which posed a difficult choice for the filmmakers: What to showcase in the film? It ultimately comes down to folding the music in with Whitney's own story—the stage she was at in her life when key songs were released and recorded. In this way, she is her music and her music is her.

"In my first meeting with the director of photography, Barry Ackroyd, I said I wanted to get close to her and that the performances would have a story," confirms Kasi Lemmons. "They're about something, and I wanted to get inside the audience's perspective, or even, if there were television cameras, those perspectives, and really get next to Whitney, particularly at certain moments. So, if we're going to have a camera on a crane, then we'd have to find an opportunity to have another camera on the stage and really look at her closely, which is super valuable in the movie. We use this technique a lot. We have both very, very big shots and very intimate shots. And I think that they're each important in telling the story of where she is emotionally when she's performing in the story of the song. I wanted to make sure that we were going to be close enough to her to feel her."

The key songs we see Whitney perform in the movie are "The Greatest Love of All," "You Give Good Love," "If You Say My Eyes Aare Beautiful," "How Will I Know," "Saving All My Love for You," "Where Do Broken Hearts Go?" "I Wanna Dance with Somebody," "Run to You," "I Will Always Love You," "The Star-Spangled Banner," "Why Does It Hurt So Bad," "'It's Not Right but It's Okay," "I'm Every Woman," "I'm Your Baby Tonight," "So Emotional," "I Didn't Know My Own Strength," "I Believe in You and Me," "I Loves You, Porgy," "And I Am Telling You I'm Not Going," and "I Have Nothing." Some songs are heard only in snippets or in montage, whereas others form part of live performances. In addition, several music videos are re-created. It all forms the rich musical mosaic of Whitney Houston's life.

Clockwise from left: Three of the iconic music videos that were re-created for the movie: "How Will I Know", "I Will Always Love You," and "It's Not Right but It's Okay."

The Choreography

James Alsop is the choreographer on the movie, having worked with such pop culture forces as Beyoncé, Jennifer Lopez, and Janelle Monáe, to name just three. James was brought in to work on . . . everything, really. But, fortunately, Alsop has been preparing for this moment most of her life.

"When I got the shooting schedule, I was like: I already know these videos, I already know these performances, when do we start dancing?!" enthuses Alsop. "My starting point was me reverting back to my nine-year-old self when I was really diving into Whitney as a performer and really getting to know all of her movements. About ten or eleven years ago, when I was finding my feet as a choreographer, there was this show where you mimic pop stars, and I was Whitney Houston! I mimicked 'I Wanna Dance with Somebody' and I performed it as if it was a live performance, with all these backup dancers behind me, and I did it! I came in about two days before the show, learned the whole thing, and I was like, I know this because it's Whitney. I've been basically living her my entire life. My starting point with this film was just reverting back to me sitting on the floor, staring at Whitney on the TV screen."

"I came in about two days before the show, learned the whole thing, and I was like, I know this because it's Whitney. I've been basically living her my entire life. My starting point with this film was just reverting back to me sitting on the floor, staring at Whitney on the TV screen."—James Alsop

Choreographer James Alsop (center) poses with the concert tour dancers.

Choreography by its very nature has to be thoroughly planned in advance, and Alsop joined the project well before shooting started, ensuring she had what she needed to do justice to the performances. "I was a part of this in July of 2021 and I wrapped in the first week of December, but after the rehearsals, there was more back and forth, as opposed to being there every day. I made sure I was there for the shoot days . . . I would say we had about three weeks of preparation, which is ample time, more than enough time to work on choreography for a Whitney Houston performance. We had two rehearsals for a number of performances, but for some even one rehearsal was sufficient. The 'How Will I Know' video was two rehearsals."

When choosing the background dancers, Alsop explains how she looked at Whitney's own choices; "In the very beginning, it was the 'America's sweetheart' story line; the backing dancers were a bunch of White people. Once she got ahold of her career—around 'I'm Your Baby Tonight'—she ended up with more male performers. Soon, there were only male performers around her. Then moving her way up from "I'm Every Woman" all the way through is when she actually took Bobby Brown's amazing choreographer, Carolyn Brown, and started hiring only Black women to perform with her, up until her My Love Is Your Love Tour. So, we really had to switch it up to mimic that. Then with her last tour, her Nothing but Love Tour, she had all males perform with her again. We really wanted to stay true to the timeline of projects."

Left: Whitney's first nationally televised performance, on the Merv Griffin Show.

Right: Filming the stripped-down, intimate "I Will Always Love You" video.

Capturing Whitney in Performance

There is a single person at the center of all this movement and excitement—Whitney Houston. No matter how big the crowd was or how many backing dancers there were, the success of any performance ultimately came down to her and her voice.

On stage, she is surrounded, yet alone. Matt Jackson likens her to an athlete about to compete. "This story is like a really great boxing movie. Like a boxer who's a prodigy, who's incredible, but we know that they have only a limited amount of time where they're going to be able to do what they do. And when you go back to the 1994 American Music Awards, it is like seeing Muhammad Ali in the Sonny Liston fight: You see him at his best. Which is why I think that was a great way for us to end the film, showing her at her peak. That's how I see it. I talked a lot about that genre, or subgenre, of Hollywood films [the sports movie]. I think that singing and performing is a full-body experience. You're using your mind, using your body, and, in this case, she's using her voice. The things that Kasi and Barry Ackroyd really focused on were the sweat and the throat and the elements of having to prepare like

Opposite: Filming the now-iconic "I Wanna Dance with Somebody" performance at the Arista Records 15th anniversary concert.

Below: Capturing the closeup at the end of a magnificent performance.

Above: Whitney performing at the Billboards American Music Awards and Naomi (*right and bottom*) capturing every nuance of that performance in the climactic final sequence of the film

RECREATING THE AMERICAN MUSIC AWARDS MEDLEY

JEFF KALLIGHERI: "We shot the American Music Awards (AMAs) at the Wang Theatre at the Boch Center in Boston. It's this great old theater in downtown, built in the 1925 and still in perfect condition. Whitney actually performed there on one of her tours."

KASI LEMMONS: "The performance that I was really looking forward to was the AMAs, when she does the medley, knowing that it's going to be at the end of the movie. We knew we were gonna have to stick the landing. I thought it would be really challenging and interesting. I had some very specifically designed shots I wanted to try . . . I brought an assistant director on who did a great job and some very thoughtful scheduling. To start off, we warmed into it, then after a couple of weeks we started doing performances. The performance section was just shy of the middle of the shoot. We got a few weeks into it and then we started doing big performances. We did several separated by a couple of days and we just had a performance set in the middle of the shoot. Then you know it's coming, so you're like 'Okay, Tampa is coming' or 'the AMAs are coming' or 'I Want to Dance with Somebody' is coming. Those three we did within two weeks."

JOHN WARHURST: "The first time we started doing recordings of Naomi singing the medley in Boston I knew she already had it down. As mentioned, not just learned it, but could embody this performance as if it were coming from her—every effort and syllable—she was so precise! This meant the main thing left to do was make sure the band that got hired was able to play this performance so naturally you wouldn't see a slip of the mask, even once. You can put mute cymbals on a drum kit, but they look so fake—they don't shimmer in the light or have all the reverberations that real cymbals do. This means the drummer and percussionist have to play for real. The positive side of this means there's a lot of power and energy on stage when filming, which is exciting for everyone, since the music on stage is at the level of the actual

performance. The way our cinematographer, Barry Ackroyd, likes to shoot is often with multiple moving cameras that could be close to the musicians, seeing hands on fretboards or keyboards, etc. This meant again that everyone needed to be on point in case the camera came close to them. We did lots of rehearsals and went through this performance step-by-step to make sure they were all comfortable with it. This can mean putting timing clicks into the track to help navigate the parts that were spontaneous in the original performance. Naomi had a brilliant movement coach [Polly Bennett], who worked through all the choreography and staging with her. It was very exciting to see it all come together in full costume and on set."

DENIS O'SULLIVAN: "When you get to that ten-minute medley at the end of the movie, watching that, in a different way from Live Aid in *Bohemian Rhapsody*, it's worth the price of admission alone. What Naomi, Kasi, Barry Ackroyd, Gerald Sullivan, and the whole team do—that sequence is so dynamic and it's so celebratory. It shows that again Clive was a hundred percent right, because he showed that to Anthony in their first meeting. I remember when Anthony sent me one of the very first outlines I read and it ended with the medley. Not yet knowing what this medley was, my note was: Shouldn't we end on 'I Will Always Love You' or one of the huge songs? Anthony said, 'No, you have to watch this to understand why this has to be the ending.' And he was right."

Right: Filming the end of the performance as Whitney looks lovingly at Cissy and baby Bobbi Kristina in the audience while the crowd goes wild.

Every aspect of Whitney's performance was important, down to the sweat on her brow (*right*) and clothing (*left*) to show the progression of Whitney's exhaustion throughout the concert tour montage. Makeup Head Tisa Howard: *"If I need a really wet 'sweat look' then I'm going to have Evian waters on standby ready to spritz her, but everything is perfectly placed so it doesn't look like it was forced. It doesn't look like it's fake. I have to think: when we sweat this is how it usually looks; we're at this level of performance or exhaustion. That's how we achieved that."*

a boxer has to spar—you have to do that as a singer. Whitney was always preparing and always getting ready for these performances, and so we show a lot of that in the film."

The glamour and authenticity of being a superstar singer, of being Whitney Houston, is on the screen. The more the unvarnished woman is visible, the more the audience can empathize with her. Tisa Howard talks about just how close the camera gets to Naomi and just how accurate the details are.

"She sweated a lot on her lip, her nose, and on her face. There's a scene in the movie where you see a montage of her performances where she starts to get exhausted and she's going from country to city to state and you're going to see the sweat progress. How we placed it looks so real. Naomi wasn't a big sweater, so I didn't have to go and pat her down a lot. If she did sweat, I'm going to use a little bit of what she has because she has a natural glow anyway, but I'm just adding to it—like some beading. I would use glycerin and a mist spray.

"There's a part where she's wearing purple with a black lapel on it. When you're really hot, you're going to have all this sweat sitting right on your chest, and you can see that on her, but the whole thing is mist that we've applied. When the light hits her you'll think, 'Oh, my gosh, she's really exhausted,' and you get it. The hair is thick onto her forehead. She's wet. If you see any old pictures of Whitney, you always see this heavy wetness around her

"She sweated a lot on her lip, her nose, and on her face. There's a scene in the movie where you see a montage of her performances where she starts to get exhausted and she's going from country to city to state and you're going to see the sweat progress. How we placed it looks so real."—Matt Jackson

nose and lips. Really sweating. I kept that in mind and made sure I hit that and Naomi had it. But she looked incredible. I've seen pictures from Naomi's performance that day and I thought, 'Holy crap, she looked like she really was in concert,' but she wasn't, of course. That was us doing it."

It is these moments that the film takes the time to stress. Everything that made Whitney who she was is evident and informs every aspect, from makeup to camerawork to Naomi's embodiment of the role.

"When she was in the studio recording 'How Will I Know,'" recalls Alsop, "that scene, which is a very special and beautiful thing, I was there just to lend some pointers to Naomi, such as on that high note, she would go crazy like this, and how that came from her gospel background. She's singing like she's in church. I would pull up the video of Whitney in the white robe at her church. This is how Whitney's seeing this recording right now because at the very beginning of her career, that's all she knew. Even if you're in a recording studio, you're still performing to a certain extent, because in those scenes she's trying to impress Clive Davis. It's magnificent to see how Naomi transformed with just those little notes and those little knickknacks, as well as performing for the huge stage and video numbers."

One of the most iconic performances of Whitney's career, singing the "Star Spangled Banner" at Super Bowl XXV. Naomi Ackie: *"There is something quite muscular about the way that she performs, given her tiny frame. You can really see the power. There were notes that Polly would give around moving her arms from her back, much like somebody who does like weightlifting or something like that. That energy comes from the spinal cord. The movements aren't just like flapping all around; whatever note comes out of her mouth and the way that her hands move has constant direction. She is not only conducting the band, but she's conducting people's emotions with it. She has so many performances where she's like literally titillating the audience."*

Above and top right: Naomi in performance.

Bottom right: The huge Naval Air Force hanger that, with the magic of special effects, would become the stage in South Africa.

Overleaf: Naomi Ackie: *"Fast forward to 'It's Not Right but It's Okay' and we've got a Whitney that is in her actual life dealing with a lot of complications. And where it's placed in the film, that song is in response to things that are going on in her actual life. Clive said something amazing which is, she has a strength and a direction and it is still to this day like an anthem for any wronged woman ever."*

RECREATING THE CONCERT FOR SOUTH AFRICA

JEFF KALLIGHERI: "We did the South Africa concert on a stage in Weymouth, Massachusetts, a former Naval Air Force location—they still have the hangar where they parked these huge fighter jets. We built a massive stage, which was very close—about 75 percent—to scale of the actual South Africa stage, because we had to shoot indoors and still make the scene work with the space we had … it was a custom stage."

JOHN WARHURST: "I would normally go up to Naomi and I'd say, just remember that when you sing you have to sing. She's got to match the energy with her face, with her look. So she has to really commit. And she said, 'I'll do that, but turn it up so loud that I can't hear myself.' We made sure we got the volume up loud enough so that she couldn't hear herself and that way she could sing at the top of her lungs and not be distracted by her own voice.

What we would often do in rehearsals as well was find ways to match performances that were spontaneous, like in South Africa. Whitney was playing South Africa to a huge crowd, and she would be feeling the moment. She would sing a lyric and then the crowd would swell up, and she'd pause, then she'd sing a little. There is no musical timing that matches what she does, so we needed to put all these beeps and clicks in so Naomi could match exactly the recording of South Africa. I think everyone probably got tired by the end of it, just hearing all these beeps and clicks throughout the whole performance every time we were filming. The drummer has to count in, but how did the drummer know when to do that count that matches the recording? The drummer then needs a count-in for the count-in! So, we gave everybody their own sound to help keep their time. The band would often have a click sound, for instance. Naomi would have a beep sound. That's how we rehearsed it. In rehearsals as well, we spent a lot of time making sure every single musician had what they needed to play perfectly in time. We went through checking that everybody had gotten all the beeps and clicks they wanted. I did that with Naomi in the studio because we would do it together, just the beeps, and then we would record her singing. … There are two recordings of everything—one during filming and one in the studio. That way we had as much material as possible to work from."

CHAPTER 7

SO EMOTIONAL
RECORDING
THE MUSIC

> 66 No one else in the world is Whitney Houston.
> You want to hear Whitney. But you want the actor
> to perform, too.... We're very blessed that Naomi's got
> an incredibly strong voice in her own right. 99
> —Josh Crook

W

hitney Houston is one of the most successful recording artists of all time. She is listed as the top-selling R&B artist of the twentieth century, with 200 million records sold. Her songs are loved the world over and sung along to by countless fans who know every note. The pressure to get her music right in the film was immense. The filmmakers wanted to give audiences a breathtaking experience, one that bears up under the scrutiny of critics, and one that hard-core fans can believe in.

With all that in mind … where did the filmmakers start?

"It is a mix of Naomi's voice and Whitney's voice," confirms Josh Crook. "No one else in the world is Whitney Houston. You want to hear Whitney. It's just like with *Bohemian Rhapsody*: It's mostly Freddie Mercury, with Rami Malek thrown in. But you want the actor to perform, too, because when it comes to taking breaths and pauses, miming doesn't quite cut it. So, we're very blessed that Naomi's got an incredibly strong voice in her own right."

The supervising music and sound editor, John Warhurst, was responsible for combining Naomi's vocals with Whitney's own archival recordings. Only this combination can be true to Naomi's performance, while also giving fans the sense that they are watching—and hearing—Whitney Houston. As Warhurst explains, "We always knew that Whitney's vocals would feature as much as possible. There aren't many singers like Whitney Houston; she's a world icon. Her vocal ability and the sound of her voice is phenomenal. Her vocal contains her spirit, if you like—which obviously needs to be part of the film. There was a general consensus that we would thread it through the film as much as we could.

"Knowing this, we started the search for as many original multitrack recordings of her songs as we needed for the film. This was quite an involved process, and the experience and contacts that the music supervisor, Maureen Crowe, had were extremely helpful in this process. Jeff James at Sony and Brandon Schmidt, who works for the Whitney Houston estate archive, were extremely helpful in this process also. It's not just a question of playing Whitney's vocal over the film and expecting people to believe it's coming from Naomi—it's not as straightforward as that. We also needed recordings of Naomi to help 'glue' Whitney's vocal to her performance and make it feel unquestionably believable. We started doing recording sessions with Naomi as soon as I arrived in Boston, gathering material and working through the performances."

Previous page: Naomi as Whitney recording another hit song.

Left, top: Whitney recording "If You Say My Eyes Are Beautiful" with Jermaine Jackson (portrayed by Jason Hunter).

Left, bottom: Getting ready to shoot the "How Will I Know" sequence in the control booth.

Below: Another day, another recording session.

> "The tracking sheets that come with the multitracks have been very helpful in working out what equipment was used on the original recordings. Also speaking to engineers who worked in the eighties about techniques and equipment has been very helpful." —John Warhurst

Working out the music at the piano (*above*) and in the studio (*right*).

The songs in the film cannot sound like cover versions. They have to sound crystal clear and up to twenty-first-century standards for theaters and home cinemas, while also retaining authenticity to the period they were originally recorded in. "The tracking sheets that come with the multitracks have been very helpful in working out what equipment was used on the original recordings," says Warhurst. "Also speaking to engineers who worked in the eighties about techniques and equipment has been very helpful. Sometimes we have audio plug-ins that do incredible simulations of that old equipment, or we just source the original equipment. Also, during the shoot, Rickey Minor lent us his bass guitar and bass synth that he played during the American Music Awards show in 1994. We used these original instruments when we filmed that performance."

Despite three decades of material to work from, there are moments in the film where there was no reference available, moments where Whitney is singing to herself or even the first big performance at Sweetwater's nightclub. For this, Warhurst and his team had to get creative and use cutting-edge technical wizardry.

"We filmed some live material during the shoot that combines Whitney's music and the live material we created on set" remembered Warhurst. "For 'The Greatest Love of All,' the script was written that at Sweetwater's, Whitney is blindsided by her mom telling her she needs to start the show as she's lost her voice. Cissy knows that Clive Davis is in the audience, so wants Whitney to sing solo. Whitney comes out on stage and is understandably nervous. She starts to sing and as she sings, she realizes not only how great her voice is, but also what affect her voice has on the audience. Here, we go from nervous Whitney to lifting-the-roof-off-the-club Whitney. When we hear Whitney's actual vocal for 'Greatest Love of All' we have only the 'lifting-the-roof-off-the-club' vocal, so it was decided Naomi should act this part in the beginning and then we would transition back to Whitney once the song takes off. We were also helped by Robbie Buchanan—the original keyboard

> "At one point in the process, John (Warhurst) messed with the mix; he said he'd found a Whitney track he didn't know he had and played it, and I was like, 'That's incredible.' Then, he says, 'That's actually Naomi.'"
>
> —Josh Crook

Naomi shows the joy of Whitney's first recording session (*right*), and an older Whitney in the struggle to get the magic back (*below*). John Warhurst: *"In her earliest days of singing her mother taught her that "You have to learn the melody first. Once you know the melody, can play the melody, sing the melody, then you can veer away from it."*

player of the single version—who played the Fender Rhodes live while Naomi sang. This live material has been blended with the multitrack recording of 'Greatest Love of All' to create a unique performance."

Because of how Whitney's voice is blended and something new is created, it wasn't a prerequisite for the movie that the lead actress could sing. But it certainly didn't hurt that Naomi Ackie has a strong voice in her own right and knows what it is to perform. "She sings really well and, like all great actors, she commits to it. In the film it's a combination of Whitney and Naomi. The fact that Naomi can sing and was up for singing meant we could do so much more in the film. We are blessed these days with audio production software that is increasingly powerful in what it can do. We can analyze what makes Whitney's vocal, in terms of which frequencies are more prevalent, the tone, and so forth, combined with what equipment was used on the original recording. We can then analyze Naomi's vocal and figure out how it's different from Whitney's. Once we know this, we can work on Naomi's vocal to make it sound closer to Whitney's. It's a bit like visual special effects, where you can change parts of the picture to what you want;

we can do this in an audio way—until we get to the point where you can't really tell the difference between the two. We did an illustration of this for 'Greatest Love of All' to show how close we can get Naomi to sound like Whitney. This was made easier, of course, by Naomi's great performance of this song."

"At one point in the process, John messed with the mix," remembers Crook. "He said he'd found a Whitney track he didn't know he had and played it, and I was like, 'That's incredible.' Then, he says, 'That's actually Naomi.'"

But it is not just about sounding right. John Warhurst's role extended to working with Naomi, Kasi Lemmons, and the director of photography, Barry Ackroyd, to ensure the

performances also looked correct. The volume of a song can be turned up as loud as they like, but if Naomi's body isn't correctly reaching for the same big note as Whitney's audio, viewers can intuitively tell it does not match. All the breakthrough computer software in the world can't make up for realism and an actual human performing naturally. If Naomi and the musicians don't believe they're really playing the songs, why should an audience?

"That was one of the things that we learned when we filmed Live Aid for *Bohemian Rhapsody*. You arrive on set and someone had put on the mute cymbals. It's like hitting a piece of wood; it just doesn't look right at all. Nobody's gonna believe that. We put the real cymbals back on, so, of course, now people start hitting real cymbals, real drums, then you have to bring the whole level of music up.... Obviously, Kasi and Barry choose the way it's going to be shot—normally, with me running on and off stage, saying, 'Guys, the mic stand is way too low for anyone. Nobody has a microphone on their chest!' But they say the shadows of the microphone are ruining the look of the face. But I'm telling them that if they have the microphone that low in order to get the nice light on the face then any musician who

> "I was asking everyone: am I doing okay? It was a constant thing of me searching for reassurance from outside of myself, and it came from Polly, Kasi, Denis, Jeff, Anthony and Clive. But also it was coming from Whitney. There were many times especially on performance days that even hearing her voice and being able to rest on the power of her voice was enough for me to melt into it and go okay, I understand." —Naomi Ackie

sees the film is going to wonder what on earth is going on with the microphone. So there was this constant thing about trying to get it so that it's a believable look. Then we get to an amusing situation where we're talking about moving the mic down, but then pointing it up a bit. 'Okay, but by how much?' Because everyone knows that a microphone comes up on the stand, fixes on, and points toward the mouth. If you put it straight in the air, like an ice-cream cone, it's gonna look weird. There were quite a lot of conversations like that."

What the incredible team of supervisors, technicians, researchers, and engineers achieved in *I Wanna Dance with Somebody* is almost a duet between Whitney and Naomi. The analogy Warhurst uses for both artists inhabiting the same aural space could not be more apt: "I always want to be able to record Naomi as much as possible and get as much material from her as possible. I also always use the same microphones so the sound matches from on set with what we recorded in the studio. The reason why is because we're going to use Whitney's vocal—we know that—but there are all kinds of other bits and pieces in Naomi's version that we steal from and borrow from, and it's what I call the 'glue.' It's like the footprint of Naomi's performance that we place Whitney Houston into.... You are hearing and watching the live part of what Naomi's doing. But every time that note comes all the way out, it's Whitney Houston singing that note. So, you get that combination of both."

Film is a fiction. It can at times be a reflection or perhaps refraction of reality, but it is not reality. In telling the story of Whitney Houston in a motion picture, the hundreds of people who have worked on it are offering fans old and new a version of the superstar that they might not have seen before. They are telling her story—no one else's. Her music and her voice were both parts of what made her unique. She chose songs that were ideally suited to her in every way, and, by simply honoring that, the film is telling her truth.

"This goes to the heart of the challenge in making a movie like this," says Anthony McCarten. "Because the songs need to tell the story. They can't just be time out, little sideshows. Where possible, they have to be integral to the emotional arc of the story you're telling. When you're lucky, as we are in Whitney's case, her music tells her story. She chose to sing songs she was feeling at the time she sang them. You have a song like 'Home'—telling us of her lifelong yearning for a safe, beautiful place, full of love—to her midmarriage songs of hurt, such as 'Why Does It Hurt So Bad,' and then the anger and defiance of 'It's Not Right but It's Okay,' to a final summing-up song like 'I Didn't Know My Own Strength.' It's all there."

CHAPTER 9

EPILOGUE
I WILL ALWAYS LOVE YOU

It has been ten years since Whitney Houston's passing, yet her music continues to touch millions of listeners and to entrance new generations of fans. The legacy of Whitney and her impact on pop culture is still being weighed.

Here, the filmmakers share their thoughts on Whitney and their hopes for the film.

PAT
HOUSTON

Producer
President/CEO, WhitNip Inc.

"You've heard many stories about Whitney
as a young girl wanting to become a teacher
or a Veterinarian. God had a different plan
and gifted her with a talent beyond words,
and her influence and Artistry transcends
all boundaries in Music. And that's what
our team will bring to audiences around the
world. John and Cissy Houston had a vision
for their daughter before anyone was there
and they succeeded beyond the distractions
that often disrupted her momentum. Clive
Davis has a vision for a film that reflects the
hard work and Artistry of an Icon. Whitney
once said to me " Sissy" I love my craft. And
I stand with this Team to produce a project
that her Fans can personally relate to
knowing the love that she had for her craft.
Her Family and her music was her home."

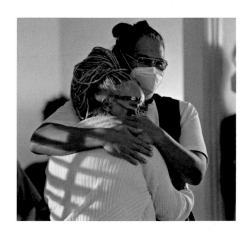

NAOMI
ACKIE

Actor, "Whitney Houston"

"She is Whitney Houston, the legend, the
Voice, America's sweetheart. But she was
also just a girl from Newark, New Jersey. For
me, my main goal in this was to play the
human being amid all the expectation and
all the pressure she dealt with. Any pressure I have is minuscule in comparison to
what she was dealing with her whole life.
It's scary, but I threw my hat in the ring. I
said 'yes.' And I lay in the bed. We worked
really hard and, hopefully, the response
reflects that."

KASI
LEMMONS

Director

"Our intention was to make a tribute. I
mean, that was our intention. Whitney was
the true north. In the 'The Greatest Love of
All' there's a line where she says 'no matter
what they take from me, they can't take
away my dignity,' and I felt she had been
stripped of some of her dignity. Some of
that was self-imposed, and some had been
caused by the insatiable media that comes
with always being in the spotlight. I wanted
to restore her dignity and have a tribute to a
very complex person, that would have
teeth –I didn't want to be too soft with it–
and emotional honesty. But that would
really remind you that this is one of the
greatest talents that ever lived. This is one
of the greatest voices there's ever been, and
for a while, she graced us with her presence. We had her, a goddess among us, and
that's something powerful to remember."

ANTHONY McCARTEN
Writer, Producer

"From Day One, Clive and I agreed on one thing: The film had to celebrate Whitney, the incomparable artist that she was. It had to focus on her music and make us realize what a once-in-a-century talent she truly was. We passed this credo down the line."

DENIS O'SULLIVAN
Producer

"To like the people who you're working with on these big, challenging films, it just makes life so much easier; and you also feel you all want to succeed together. I want so desperately for Clive and Pat to be happy and for all of us to be celebrating at the premier and saying, 'Oh, my God, we did it.' And Whitney would be sitting next to Pat, happy."

JOSH CROOK
Executive Producer

"This was meant to be a celebration of Whitney's life and her music; her career and her triumphs. This is not a tabloid- or a gossip-column thing, like she had to deal with her whole life. This was meant to focus on the real-life, human stuff we all deal with, and some of us come to it at different times than others. It was meant to be a celebration of this incredible woman and everything she accomplished."

JEFF KALLIGHERI
Producer

"Movies are like miracles when they come together, against impossible odds, and this one is no different. I genuinely believe that throughout this process we were getting help. At every turn when things could have gone wrong, they went right. And I can't explain it. All I can say is we were so lucky to have had the chance to tell this once-in-a-lifetime story about one of the greatest of all time, Whitney Houston. It felt like she was with us the entire way and Naomi was the conduit to let her shine one more time."

BRIAN BADIE
Hair Department Head

"I succeeded as a hairstylist in the way I wanted to represent Whitney. I am definitely proud of what I did and accomplished. I'm excited to see the final product."

MATT JACKSON
Producer

"This movie is about a genius of song and wanting to showcase her genius. We know what her challenges were in life, and we all have challenges and vices and personal issues. We know that, that's sort of baked into the cake, but for younger generations and for people who love Whitney—and there are so many people who love her out in the world—we wanted to do right by her. We wanted to show her without neutering the story or neutering what actually happened. We wanted to tell a story about how unique of an individual and singer she was in the most entertaining but substantive way."

LAWRENCE MESTEL
Producer
Founder and CEO, Primary Wave

"Whitney Houston was America's Princess. The voice of a generation. Possibly the greatest voice of our time. She was incomparable, uniquely gifted, and a warm heart and soul. This movie is about shinning the spotlight on her once again and showing the world and reminding her fans, what a supremely unparalleled artist Whitney was. This will be the one authorized biographical film that the Houston Family and Clive Davis have jointly participated in and provides a true historical perspective as told by the pen of the Oscar-nominated writer Anthony McCarten."

JAMES ALSOP
Choreographer

"I hope that fans, old and new, will take away from the film a sense of compassion and a sense of understanding. There's just so much that goes into a performer's life beyond the glitz and glam of performing, red carpets, and events, and all that. I truly hope the fans understand the uniqueness of the gift that was Whitney Houston and her voice; the uniqueness and the power that she commanded with her presence on stage, and that they understand how special and how much all of that meant to her while she was here and how she truly gave us her all as a performer. She gave us everything she had in her arsenal, and I do not think we'll ever get another artist like her. I just hope the audience understands how special she was."

BLACK LABEL MEDIA
Producers

"You get a look at Whitney that people have never seen before. You'll get to walk away celebrating her, which I think is what audiences love. You're able to go on the ride with her, be a part of her climb, and that's a really satisfying experience."

KIM COLEMAN
Casting Director

"You get a look at Whitney that people have never seen before. You'll get to walk away celebrating her, which I think is what audiences love. You're able to go on the ride with her, be a part of her climb, and that's a really satisfying experience."

TISA HOWARD
Makeup Department Head

"You see this woman who is beautiful. There is something relatable to everyone [about her] and you can take one little thing and make it personal for you. That's how I felt. You see the strength, regardless of whether you knew about her pain. I think this movie has given me more understanding for her, and even more respect. I got to look inside out, get more compassion about her and more empathy. There are some parts that we laughed or we saw the cry for help but we missed it. I wish she could see how much people loved her and appreciated her. And, you know what, even in her weakest moments, she was still strong to me. She has stood the test of time."

JOHN WARHURST
Supervising Sound Editor

"There are two main reasons her music endures. First, it's her vocal, the sound of her voice and incredible vocal ability. Second, it's the quality of her songs. You put these two things together, and they create something that endures. Iconic singers often have a unique quality to the sound of their voices, which is much more than just being able to hit the notes. It's often a tonal quality that allows people, after hearing the voice for just a few seconds, to know exactly who is singing. Whitney had all of these things in abundance, which is why people still listen to her records to this day. As soon as she comes on the radio, most people will know after just a few seconds—that's Whitney!"

DAYSHA BROADWAY

Editor

"There can be an overwhelming weight to telling the story of someone's life and it gets even trickier when that person is Whitney Houston, a beloved icon with deep complexities. During my work on the film, it was my goal to tell her story as elegantly as possible and in celebration of her life.

"For decades, Whitney gave us everything she had. She threw herself into every performance, belting that phenomenal voice, sweating up a storm, and telling us a story through her music! She gave everything she had and her gift was an aid to so many people. As the editor, I knew I'd have to do the same for her: give it everything I have. I tried to pull on any moment, that Naomi so beautifully expressed, which would allow us to feel her perspective. I wanted the audience to truly experience the many sides of this beautiful, complicated woman. Hopefully, the film reflects that."

CHARLESE ANTOINETTE JONES

Costume Designer

"I'm hoping that people will watch this movie and realize, 'Oh, right, this is Whitney, and this is why she was as big as she was.' She deserves some respect."

JANINA LEE

Makeup Department Head, Whitney Houston's Makeup Artist

"Working on a movie showcasing Whitney's legacy, whom I had the pleasure of having a personal relationship with and who has impacted my life beyond measure, was a complete honor and full-circle moment for me.

"Whitney was dedicated to her music, family, and fans and often loyal to a fault. As many saw through the eyes of the media, and what we see in the movie, I saw intimately, life hit her hard countless times. We also saw that she remained stable due to God, her incredible gift, and dedication to us all.

"She had an inner strength and resilience that kept her going and she channeled that into every note, song, and performance. Many moments while filming left me speechless and I just hope what we accomplished gives everyone a better understanding of Whitney."

CLIVE DAVIS

Producer
Chief Creative Officer,
Sony Music Entertainment

"From all my experience with Whitney,
I knew her story had not yet been told.
Anthony McCarten and I were committed
to a musically rich screenplay that reveals
more of her character and life. This is the
full biopic of Whitney Houston. My mission
was to make a no-holds-barred film–a very
realistic and very honest story. Whitney
was a musical genius, whose life was full
of dreams for herself as well as personal
battles. The movie *I Wanna Dance with
Somebody* will also show why she
was–and is–loved by millions.
This is special and unique, like Whitney."

ACKNOWLEDGMENTS

The Estate of Whitney E. Houston would like to thank all of the participants involved in the process of this amazing project. I think it's safe to say that we all were in love with this amazing songstress Whitney Houston.

Bearing in mind that it takes a village to create such a memoir that's authentic to its subject, writing these acknowledgments can be somewhat difficult because you want everyone involved to feel appreciated. I'd like to first thank Robert Dippold from Primary Wave for the introduction to Roger Shaw from Weldon Owen. Roger's team undoubtedly took their marching orders and created and outlined a book to reflect the life of a legend produced by producing partners Clive Davis, Larry Mestel, Denis O'Sullivan, Jeff Kalligheri, and Anthony McCarten.

Clive Davis! Thank you for continuing to embrace Whitney's legacy with the passion that she deserves. You have definitely been the force behind the creation of this project. With much gratitude and appreciation, I thank you for the higher level of consciousness that you have brought to Whitney's story. Larry Mestel—definitely the balancing act. My life totally changed when I met you. Thank you for your countless acts of professionalism for every situation encountered. Your strong sense of leadership came at the right moments during this production. Jeff and Denis, your participation has always been seamless—regardless of any obstacles or challenges, you always manage to make things right. Much love to both of you. And of course, The Maestro Anthony McCarten—thank you for putting together such a diverse group of producers and a director who was focused on the highlights of a star destined for greatness. When you're planning such a project of this magnitude, you have to find all the right acts. and you managed it very well. You stepped back to be the eye-catcher for it all and you move quietly and effectively. Thank you. Kasi Lemmons and team— Thank you for stepping in and doing what you do. The challenges I'm sure were great but you hung in and gave what a director should do, and that's follow the vision that everyone anticipated to produce a great story that only Whitney would approve. Thank you to Sony Pictures who collected many of the assets and images for this book.

Thank you to Naomi Ackie for meeting the challenge by discussing the magic she felt being involved with this film. It was definitely a pleasure to have all the interviews from the other cast members and crew. Your words of delight for our dear Whitney more than honored her legacy. To Black Label—your involvement has been a blessing to this project. And last but certainly not least—to the Whitney Houston Estate family. The historians behind the legend—thank you for always stepping up and continuing to represent the legacy that you have been so proud of since the beginning of Whitney's career. The music business has been our life for over thirty-plus years. Dedicated and proving to be Whitney's flame-keepers—Donna Houston, Lynne Volkman, and Ulysses Carter—I owe the most to you. I shed tears of joy for your incomparable love for the work you do for Whitney's legacy. You work tirelessly on everything Whitney. Donna Houston—your care for this book has made this project easy to accomplish. Thank you for always coming through—love you more than you know. Ulysses—I can't ignore your loyalty to your work—thank you for everything Houston. You have been exemplary, and you always made Whitney proud. Lynn Volkman! My Volkman!—your loyalty extends beyond professionalism. Your longtime friendship is so appreciated, and I have always appreciated every effort that you have given above and beyond the call of duty. Thank you, my friend.

To our Estate Partner Primary Wave—where do I begin?. You have made Whitney's legacy such an enjoyable journey. Your initiation of this book project along with Compelling Pictures is just another key unlocking the promises of what's to come. You are treasured because of your constant understanding of Whitney's Legacy. Thank you for your dedication and guidance, leadership, friendship, and family bond. The Houston Family is more than blessed that all of you are part of such a remarkable talent—Whitney Houston!

Pat Houston, Producer
President/CEO, *WhitNip Inc.*
Executor

PICTURE CREDITS

All images that appear in this book are courtesy Sony Tristar, with the exception of the following:

Key: R=right; L=left; T=top; B=bottom)

Alamy Stock Photo: Doug Peters 25; **Media Punch Inc.** 10, 11B; **Zuma Press Inc.** 11T; **Courtesy of Charlese Antoinette:** 61R, 104TL, 104B; **Estate of Whitney Houston:** 19, 97B; **Getty Images: Frederic Reglain/Gamma-Rapho Collection** 7, **Ebet Roberts/Premium Archive** 43L; **Shutterstock: Matt Baron/BEI** 15; **Mark J. Terrill/AP** 144TL; **Olga Sukhotinskaya:** 105, 113L, 113R.

For more information about Whitney, please visit www.WhitneyHouston.com.

The film *I Wanna Dance with Somebody* was produced by the following:

weldon**owen**

an imprint of Insight Editions
P.O. Box 3088
San Rafael, CA 94912
www.weldonowen.com

CEO Raoul Goff
VP Publisher Roger Shaw
Editorial Director Katie Killebrew
Senior Editor Karyn Gerhard
VP Creative Chrissy Kwasnik
Art Director Allister Fein
VP Manufacturing Alix Nicholaeff
Sr Production Manager Joshua Smith
Sr Production Manager, Subsidiary Rights Lina s Palma-Temena

Design by Roger Gorman, Reiner Design Consultants, Inc.

Weldon Owen would like to thank Jeff Kalligheri and Matteo Coelho at Compelling Pictures; Roxy Campos at Sony for
her work with the images; the cast and crew who so graciously gave of their time to be interviewed; Simon Ward who
so expertly pulled it all together; the tireless work of Kayla Belser, copyeditor Margaret Parrish, and proofreader Bob
Cooper; and finally the wonderful designer Roger Gorman, who made it all look so beautiful.

Text © 2022 Weldon Owen International

ISBN: 978-1-68188-919-1

Manufactured in China by Insight Editions
10 9 8 7 6 5 4 3 2

Insight Editions, in association with Roots of Peace, will plant two trees for each tree used in the manufacturing of
this book. Roots of Peace is an internationally renowned humanitarian organization dedicated to eradicating land
mines worldwide and converting war-torn lands into productive farms and wildlife habitats. Roots of Peace will plant
two million fruit and nut trees in Afghanistan and provide farmers there with the skills and support necessary for
sustainable land use.